The Ultimate BONSAI HANDBOOK

The Complete Guide for Beginners

Yukio Hirose

TUTTLE Publishing

Tokyo | Rutland, Vermont | Singapore

Contents

CHAPTER 3

BONSAI ACCORDING TO PLANT CATEGORY

Shouhaku

Zouki

Hanamono

Mimono

Kusamono

INTRODUCTION

Bonsai is a part of Japanese culture that has long been in the world's spotlight. I discovered bonsai when I was a junior in college. After finishing up a karate training workshop in Kochi Prefecture, I headed over to the Osaka World Expo (1970). When I first laid eyes on authentic bonsai, I was moved by their beauty and decided then and there to make bonsai my career. My family already had a nursery and a decent landscape at home, so while I was helping out with the family business, I was fostering bonsai. Eventually, I started selling bonsai as well.

I've reached this point in my career without having any formal training. I just imitate what I see. "Those whose knowledge exceeds mine are my masters." "Learn a little something each day." That's how I decided to go about it, and it's how I amassed my knowledge of bonsai and my skill in growing them. I found myself completely absorbed by the world of bonsai, and by this wonderful process of taming miniature trees on the palms of my hands. Before I knew it, half a century had gone by.

Miniature bonsai don't require high quality, aged materials. You can start with materials you have at hand, cutting, dividing, pruning, and shaping with wire. With a little determination, you can create your own piece.

For beginners who've just opened the door to the world of bonsai, this book will guide you through it, step by step, with visuals to help you along the way. Start by observing and imitating. Once you become fairly well acquainted with bonsai, you can start experimenting with your own ideas.

In recent years, raising bonsai has become a hobby for people of all ages, in many parts of the world. I hope that this book will help add to the number of bonsai practitioners, and spread the love of bonsai.

Yukio Hirose

CHAPTER 1
THE BASICS

DIFFERENCES BETWEEN BONSAI AND GARDENING

Even though the same plant can be used in both container gardening and bonsai, the goal, technique, container and result will be different.

In bonsai, the role of the pot is perhaps more complex than it is for container gardening. The pot is shallow and must harmonize with the plant's gender attributes. The pot's size should be proportionate to the tree's height, trunk width, root system and foliage. Shape is another point of difference between container gardening and bonsai. In gardening, the plants are deeper-rooted, grow upwards, and spread out in a natural dome. Bonsai, on the other hand, utilizes various techniques to train the trunk, branches and roots to replicate the form and features of an aged tree. Even the tiniest bonsai inspires a certain reverence. When you look at a bonsai, it should seem as if it has lived for centuries. It's not just a miniature in the natural world; its venerable appearance makes it seem also connected to the spiritual world.

MEMO

Bonsai are classified by the height of the tree

Large-size (also called Imperial) bonsai if the height is taller than 23¾ in (60 cm).

Medium-size bonsai if the height is between 8 and 15¾ in (20 and 40 cm).

Small-size bonsai if the height is lower than 8 in (20 cm). *They are usually about the size of a hand's palm. This book will introduce small-size bonsai.

Bean-size bonsai if the height is lower than 4 in (10 cm).

WHAT TO OBSERVE IN A BONSAI

The following tips can help you better observe and appreciate bonsai. Your first look should be up close; then, slowly distance yourself from the tree until you can see it in its entirety and context. Going to exhibitions will give you an excellent opportunity to observe a wide variety of bonsai. These pointers will help you determine if each part of the bonsai is in good shape:

7 TREE CROWN
The crown should have a semicircular shape.

6 BRANCH ARRANGEMENT
The branches should be arranged in a uniform way.

5 TRUNK'S ARRANGEMENT
The trunk should be upright and grow slender toward the branches.

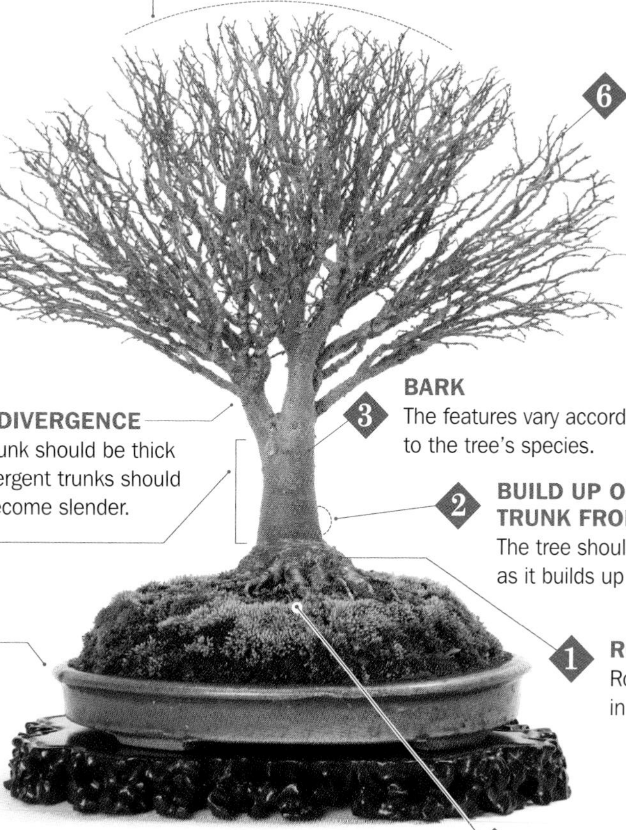

4 TRUNK'S DIVERGENCE
The main trunk should be thick and the divergent trunks should gradually become slender.

3 BARK
The features vary according to the tree's species.

2 BUILD UP OF THE TRUNK FROM THE ROOT
The tree should get tougher as it builds up from roots to trunk.

9 POT MATCHING
The pot should be chosen according to the tree species.

1 ROOTS
Roots should spread in every direction.

Keyaki, Japanese Zelkova

8 PLANTING POSITION
There should be a balance between the tree and the pot.

10 FLOWERS/FRUITS
There should be a noticeable balance to the distribution of blooming flowers or fruits on the tree.

Juugatsu Sakura

Binankazura

Among the types of bonsai, other than Shouhaku, Zouki, Hanamono and Mimono, there are also Kusamono, which are planted alongside other bonsai.

Kuromatsu

Shouhaku

Starting from Matsu, Zugi, Hinoki and other evergreen coniferous trees are called Shohaku. Overflowing with life energy, they have the charm that comes with longevity, surfaces that attest to many years of living. Among them, Matsu are often used as New Year decorations, due to their color, which is said to bring luck (pictured here is a Kuromatsu—Black pine).

Zouki

Trees ranging from broad-leaved deciduous trees, such as Momiji, Keyaki and Ichou, to broad-leaved evergreens such as Kuchinashi and Isozanshou, are called Zouki. Each year they pass through the cycle of the four seasons.

Yamamomiji

Hanamono

Tsubaki, Ume, Sakura, Satsuki and other flower-producing trees are called Hanamono. They require special care in the pruning of the flower sprouts.

Tsubaki

Mimono

Species that produce fruits, such as Rouyagaki. Akebi, Karin and so on, are called Mimono. Each tree species follows a different breeding process.

Rouyagaki

Kusamono

Trees that produce grass, such as Daimonjisou, Sumire and Yukinoshita, are called Kusamono. These can be planted in combination with other bonsai in the same pot.

Daimonjisou

TREE SHAPES

Tree shapes are chosen well in advance in order to be formed perfectly over time. By knowing all the different shapes, you'll have a better sense of what works, and can plan how to shape your tree accordingly.

Chokkan

A single trunk grows upright, its straight branches stretching toward the sky. Its simplicity gives it a strong, immediate presence.

Soukan

This bonsai has two trunks growing from its roots. The main and secondary trunks together give Soukan a sense of rhythm.

Shakan

This type has a single trunk growing diagonally. It has dense branches on all sides.

Moyogi

The trunk and branches grow in a wave-like pattern (left to right or front to back). Its beauty comes from the intriguing movement in its curves.

Kengai

The trunk grows lower than the bottom of the pot, dipping below its edge. If the trunk does not dip below the edge of the pot it's called a Hankengai (Half kengai).

Fukinagashi

The trunk and branches look as if they have collapsed naturally from the force of wind. The beauty of this tree comes from the long branches stretching sideways.

BunJingi

A slender trunk grows long, and lower branches are cut. During the Edo period, this shape was popular among BunJin (literary people), hence the name BunJingi (BunJin's Tree).

Kabutachi

Multiple trunks grow from the roots. The beauty of this shape lies in the balance between the main trunk and the secondary ones.

Ishitsuki

This type of bonsai is grown atop natural stone with the help of keto soil.

Neagari

The roots grow visibly on top of the soil. It has a rough appearance, as its roots look as if they have been exposed to violent forces of nature.

Yoseue

Multiple trees grow in a single pot. It looks like a full forest or landscape in miniature.

INSTRUMENTS USED FOR BONSAI TREATMENT

When starting a bonsai, arrange your instruments first. Using the appropriate tool for each task is the first step in creating bonsai.

Pruning scissors for cutting slender branches.

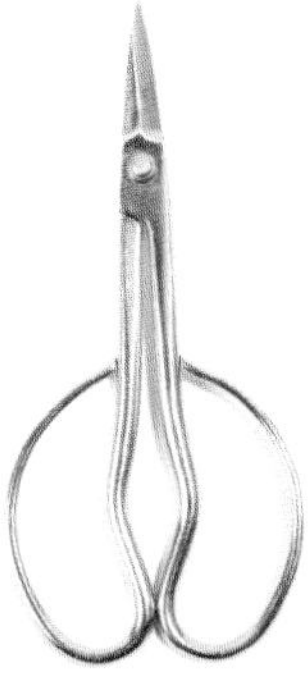

Rooting scissors for cutting roots while transplanting and for cutting thick branches.

Tongs for bending and removing wire.

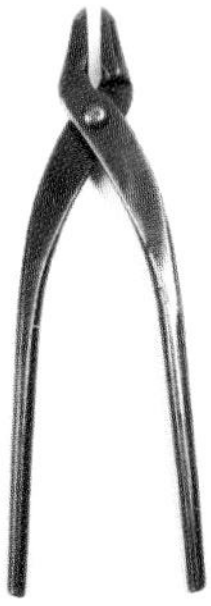

Wire cutters (large, medium and small sizes)
Choose the size according to the thickness of the wire.

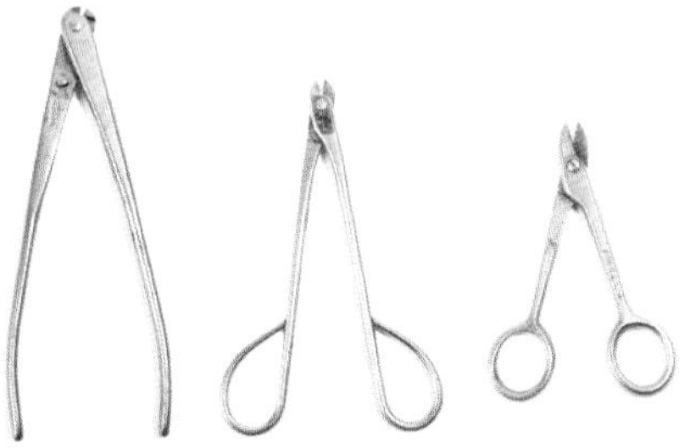

Leaf cutter for cutting leaves.

Rotating table for rotating the tree while working on it.

Branch-cutting scissors for cutting roots or thick branches.

Rake for scooping and loosening branches during transplanting.

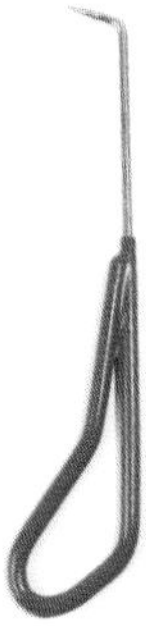

Pliers for bending wires during transplanting.

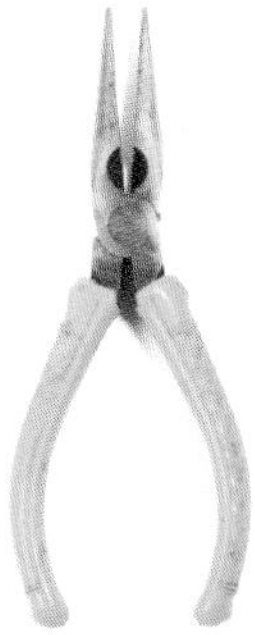

Saw for cutting thick trunks.

Palm broom for cleaning the rotating table and other surfaces.

Tweezers for plucking or arranging sprouts.

Carving knife for creating Jin or Shari.

Copper/aluminum wire for fixing netting to the bottom of a pot, fixing the tree, and more. The thickness runs from 0.3 to 0.8 mm, depending on the need.

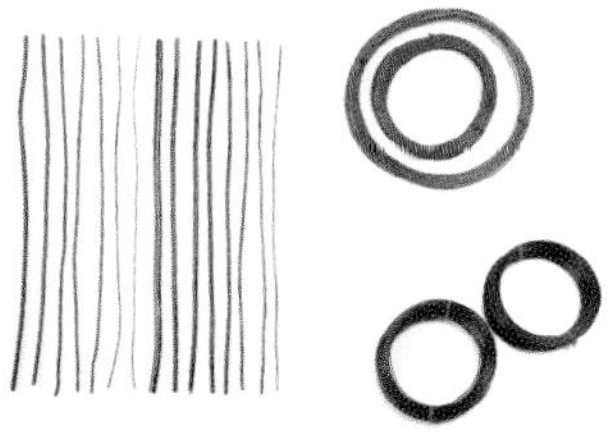

Bamboo skewer for filling gaps in the soil.

Scalpel used during the Yobitsugi process.

Spray bottle for cleaning the pot during transplanting, and for spritzing leaves, flowers and so on.

Soil receptacle for spreading soil in the pot.

Net for the bottom of the pot for preventing insects from getting into the soil from beneath and the soil from spilling out.

Watering can Use one with a long spout for better reach, when needed. Use the smaller nozzle to direct water where needed.

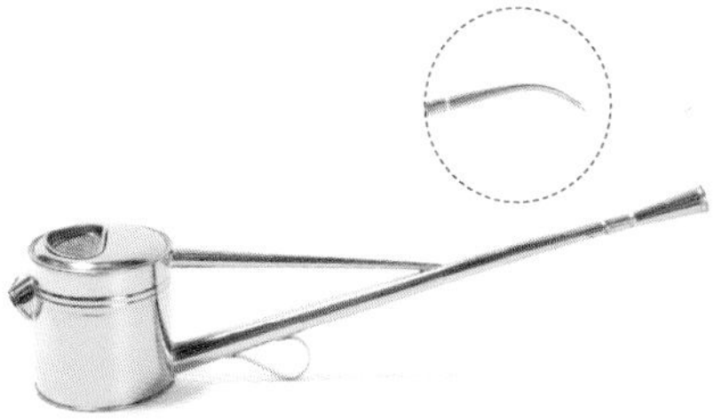

TYPES OF SOIL

The most commonly used soil is a combination of akadama and river sand. Kanuma soil is usually used for Satsuki; river sand and bamboo charcoal are used for Shohaku.

1 Akadama small grain 70%; river sand 30%.

2 Akadama medium grain 70%; river sand 30%.

3 River sand.

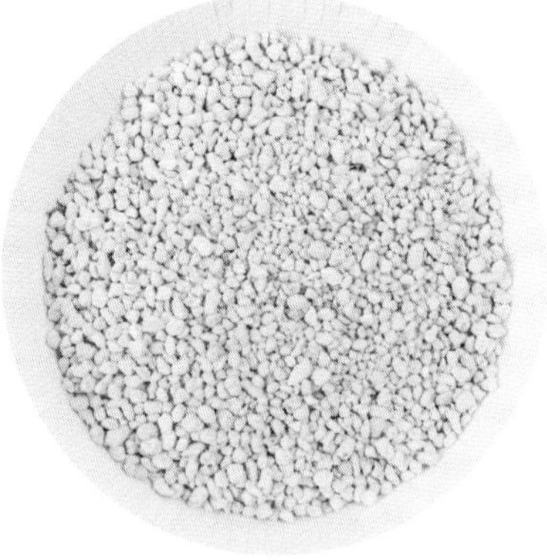

4 Kanuma small grain.

5 Bamboo charcoal.

HOW TO MAKE KETO SOIL

Keto soil is a clay-like soil, rich in nutrients. It is sticky and usually used in Ishitsuki or when applying moss to bonsai. This soil will always dry easily and shrink in size, so mix it with akadama. When making keto soil, adding akadama to the mix causes the soil to absorb more moisture and harden more firmly, whereas adding more keto makes it softer. Mix the two so that it's just as firm as needed.

1 Prepare the soil. Akadama small grain 30%; keto soil 70%.

2 Put the keto soil in a container, add enough water, and start mixing the soil with your hand.

3 Add the akadama and keep mixing.

TIP

Make it hard enough so that when the soil is placed on one side of the container, the bottom of the container remains visible.

4 Keep mixing until it starts to become sticky.

5 Roughly shaping it into a ball will make it easier to use.

TYPES OF BONSAI POTS

Bonsai use special types of pots. In the past, Chinese pots were the most commonly used containers, but more recently Japanese pots, with their serene patterns, have gained the spotlight.

Deimono

This is the most common pot for Shouhaku. The pot gives an impression of strength and enhances the green color of the leaves. Its appeal lies in its simple textures and natural tones.

Shudei Sotoen Chouhou

Shudei Sotoen Seihou

Shudei Sotoen Maru

Shidei Kenmokkou Shiki

Shudei Mokkou Shiki

Hakudei Kittate Daen

Irobachi (Colored/Glazed Pots)

Usually used for species that are not Shouhaku. They come in all colors. If used with Hanamono or Mimono, match the color of the pot with the color of the flowers or fruits.

Aokouchi Kittate Maru

Chinyuu Daen

Keiketsuyuu Mokkou Shiki

Kinyuu Nadekaku Chouhou

Chiriyuu Mokkou Shiki

Kusakinyuu Nadekaku Chouhou

Youhen Kittate Seihou

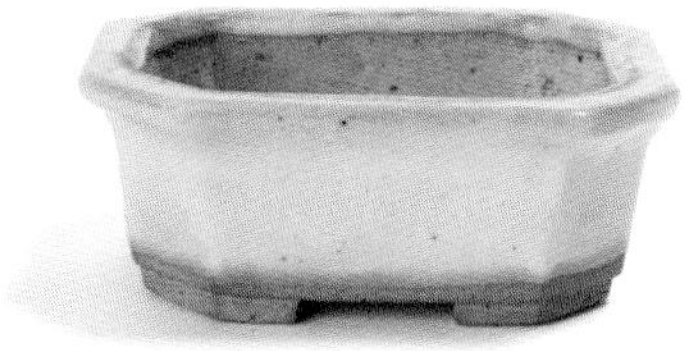

Hakuyuu Sumikiri Chouhou

Oukinyuu Sotoen Maru

Edzuke Hachi (Ceramic Painting)

These pots have beautiful paintings, but for beginners, it's very difficult to choose an Edzuke Hachi that matches with their tree. However, if well matched with the tree and the shelf decor, they can enhance the overall setting tremendously.

Iroe Sansuizu Chouhou

Iroe Hanazu Chouhou

Akae Sansuizu Chouhou

Koudei Sometsue Seihou

Sometsuke Sansuizu Maru

Ouyuu Hanazu Rokkaku

Kawari Hachi

Despite their irregular shapes, they have a truly unique style, one that does not conform to rules. Using them could end up being a nice new discovery.

Oosumiiri Seihou

Ruri Tanzaku Daen

Shinsha Sotoen Maru

Youhen Kahou Seihou

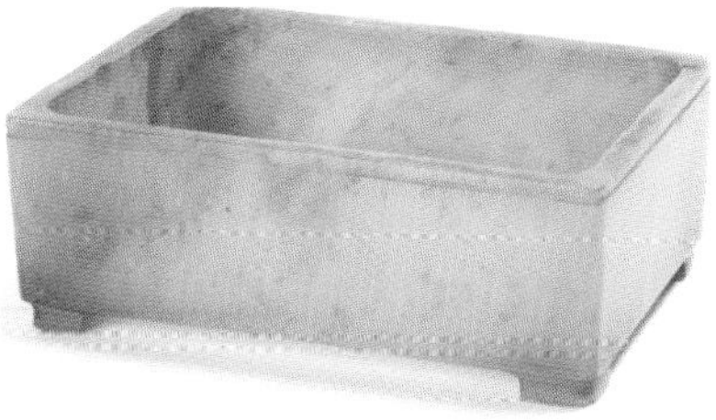

Menou Kurinuki Chouhou

Bizen Takebushi Maru

Keiketsuyuu Chouhou

DISPLAY STANDS FOR BONSAI

Bonsai are different from ornamental plants. They are placed indoors only rarely on the days when they are the most beautiful. On those days, we place the bonsai on decorative shelves, desks or ground plates.

Decorative Shelves

There are two and three-shelf fixtures. Shelves with a wide difference in height are called "Difference shelves." There are also semicircular shelves, with plenty of varieties to choose from. Some examples of shelves are:

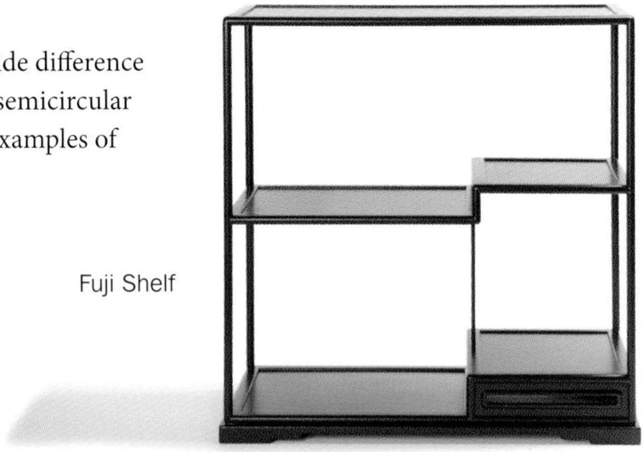

Fuji Shelf

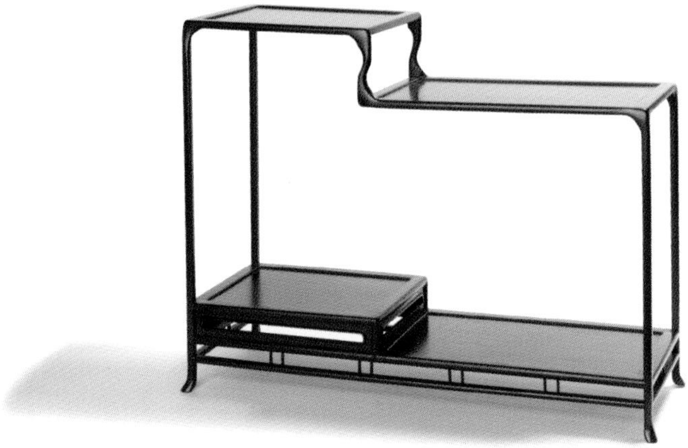

Rokko Shelf

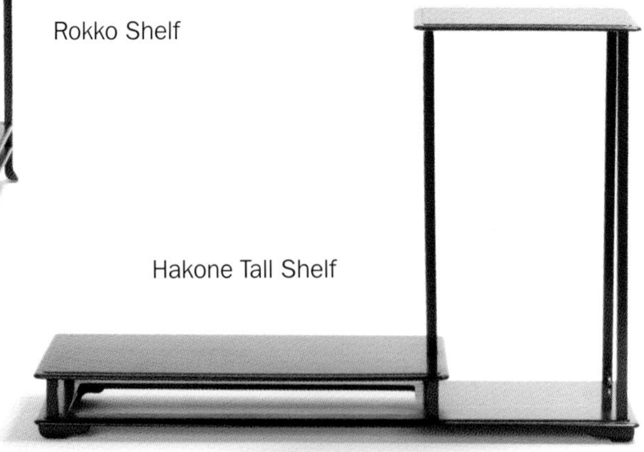

Hakone Tall Shelf

Warabi Shelf

Mikadzuki Shelf

Tables

These are usually used for special bonsai, to which we match a shelf of the right height. In the case of Kengai or other situations where the branches are low, use a tall table.

Shitan Tenzenkei Table (Natural carving table)

Marukou Table (Tall round table)

Tall Table

Maruko Table (Short round table)

Sangi Table (Abacus table)

Ground Plates

These are ground boards where we place the bonsai. We choose the board according to the size of the bonsai and the atmosphere we want to give to it.

Tenzenki Plate

Maru Plate (Round plate)

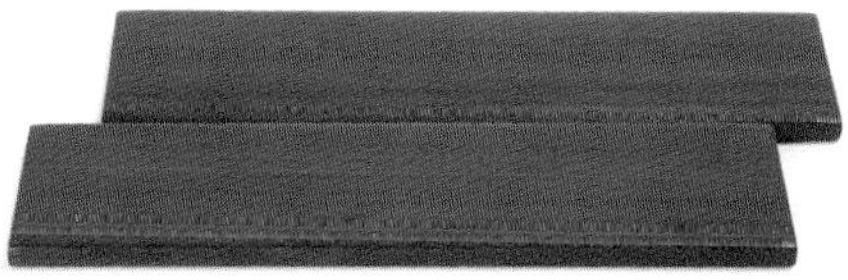

Urushi Plate

Accessories

Many simple small accessories, such as figures of people, animals, buildings and more, can be spread around the tree. You can find accessories made of ceramic, wood and metal in all shapes, or use some that are both suitable for the bonsai and meaningful to you.

HOW TO PLACE BONSAI

Let's try to place a grown bonsai on the flower beds. There is "shelf decorating" for decorative shelves and "floor decorating" for the floor.

Shelf Decorating

In their role as protagonist trees, Shohaku are usually placed on the center of top shelves, generally along with Kusamono. Actually, when placed near growing grass, the grass will naturally congregate in a small space.

Shelf decoration with five bonsai

Upper shelf: Shinpaku
Lower shelf (from the right): Yukemomo, Nirekeyaki
On the floor (from the left): Zumi, Hinasou

Shelf decoration with five bonsai

Upper shelf: Shinpaku
Middle shelf: Miyasama Kaede
Lower shelf: Himitsu Kimisou
On the floor (from the left): Keyaki, Sumire

Shelf decoration with seven bonsai

Upper shelf: Shinpaku
Middle shelf (from the right): Tsuyama Hinoki, Choujubai
Lower shelf (from the right): Chirimenkazura, Kaede
On the floor (from the left): Sarusuberi, Hari Inunazuna

Floor Decorating

Place the bonsai on the floor. Align the main tree and the secondary trees to the three points dictated by a hanging scroll. Make sure that the main tree is aligned with the axis of the three points.

Example (from the left) Shinpaku, Tokiwahimehagi, Kaede

Modern Decorating

In designs that are not classic, place the trees in an innovative way. In this example, we went for a cross shape and tried to break up the overall symmetry a bit.

Example: Upper shelf: Shinpaku
Middle shelf (from the left): Kuchinashi, Buronzuhime, Tsuyama Hinoki
Lower shelf: Otomegi Boushi

column 1

Where to Buy Bonsai?

If you are thinking of buying a bonsai, there are three main ways to obtain one.
1. Buying through a specialty bonsai store. Often these stores have considerable variety, and may also offer classes on bonsai care and maintenance. Also, customers can bring in their bonsai for special care or treatment of specific conditions and so on.
2. Buying from a bonsai exhibition. These offer an opportunity to appreciate up close some well-done bonsai and study them in more depth. Often, bonsai are offered for sale at these exhibitions, which means you can examine them yourself and choose according to your own taste. The sellers are subject experts and can offer advice on growing and caring for the bonsai.
3. Buying from the Internet. There are plenty of online stores where you can easily get any species of bonsai. Check out several vendors. Customer reviews can be helpful when choosing where to buy.
Remember that an important step in the selection of bonsai choosing the pot. The relationship between tree and pot cannot be overemphasized. If you take care of the tree from the very first step, you'll deepen your relationship with your bonsai.

2

3

1

1. At an exhibition sale, you'll find both young and mature trees.
2. Exhibition sales offer a one-stop opportunity to see myriad bonsai.
3. Bonsai specialty stores are great sources of information as well as of bonsai.

CHAPTER 2

BONSAI MAINTENANCE AND CARE

BASIC MANAGEMENT

When a bonsai is in its best possible environment, it can remain a healthy and beautiful, and be a part of your life for many years.

1 CHOOSING THE PLACEMENT

In general, a tree's environment should be well-ventilated and provide direct sunlight. However, depending on the species, the placement can vary. For most bonsai, it's recommended to have a dedicated shelf in the garden. Only the upper section should be dry, due to sunlight, whereas the bottom part should stay dark enough to remain moist. You can commission shelves from bonsai vendors.

Alternatively, you can also raise a bonsai even on a balcony or veranda. In that case, to protect the pot from being blown away, protective rubber or special pots will be needed.

Depending on the species, some trees need different treatment according to the different seasons. Species that are vulnerable to summer conditions should be moved to cooler places, avoiding direct sunlight, and species that are vulnerable to winter should be taken indoors and kept warm.

By choosing a good location according to the nature of the plant, flower and fruit quality can be vastly improved and diseases can be avoided, thus leading to a strong and robust tree.

2 WATERING

It is said that "breeding a bonsai means giving water for three years." Watering is a simple task, but requires more thought than many people realize. Generally, when the surface of the pot is dry, the plant should receive enough water to overflow from the pot. However, depending on the species, some trees prefer either more or less than that amount.

The quantity of water should differ according to the season and the plant's status.

You can generally spray tap water with a hose; however, if the pot is too dry you should use a watering can. This method is more focused, and allows you to better observe the bonsai's condition and estimate the best timing for each action item, such as checking the bonsai's fertility and determining any need for weeding, fertilizing or removal of metal wires.

If for any reason your bonsai has gone too long without water, you can use the immersion/soaking method of "first aid" by placing the pot in a basin of water, allowing it to absorb through the bottom as well as the top of the pot. If it's a summer evening, you can refresh your bonsai by sprinkling water on the leaves.

Soaking is quick first aid for a parched bonsai. Immerse the pot to the base of the tree.

3 FERTILIZING

In case of bonsai, the fertilizer is generally a pellet type that resembles small stones/pebbles. These are usually placed on the upper section of the soil and wired into place. Deciding whether to apply fertilizer or determining what fertilizer to use depends on the tree species. Hanamono (bonsai with flowers or fruits) require special fertilizer. Also, when placing two or more fertilizer pellets, give some thought to their arrangement so as to maintain balance.

♦ HOW TO FERTILIZE

TIP
Cutting the wire diagonally will make it easier to push the wire in the soil.

1 Wrap wire around the fertilizer pellet.

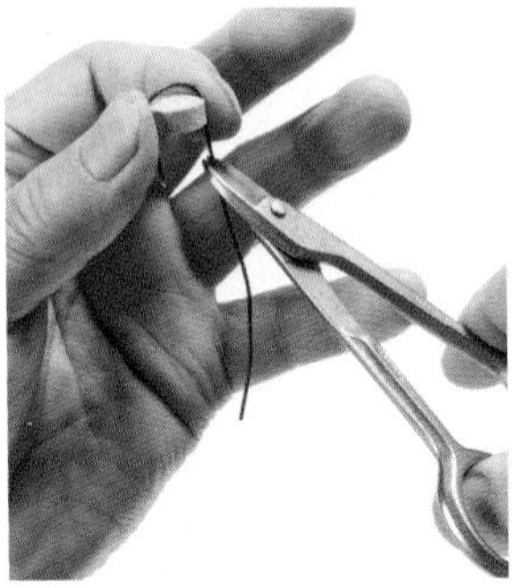

2 Cut the wire with scissors and align the ends before bending so that the sides are of equal length.

TIP
For Hanamono, phosphoric acid or potassium-based fertilizers are the most commonly used. In the case of Rouyagaki, such as the one pictured on the left, the fertilizer should be placed on opposite sides.

TIP
In the case of Shohaku (evergreens), using nitrogen-based fertilizer will cause the leaves to grow in a wonderful shade of green.

3 Push the ends around both sides of the pellet to anchor it to the soil.

♦ TYPES OF FERTILIZER

Large Organic Fertilizer (oil cake) nitrogen rich

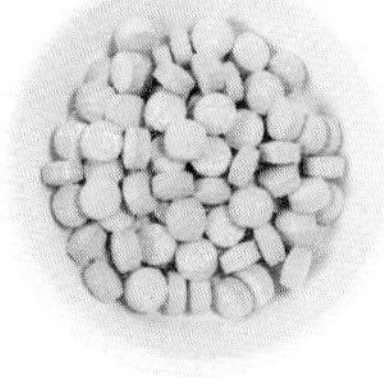

Small Organic Fertilizer (chicken poultry manure) rich in phosphoric acid

Specific Fertilizer for growing better flowers or fruits, rich in phosphoric acid and potassium, slow acting

Standard Fertilizer (composite fertilizer)
*Laid down before other fertilizers

Slow/Mild Fertilizer (composite fertilizer)
*Lasts for two months

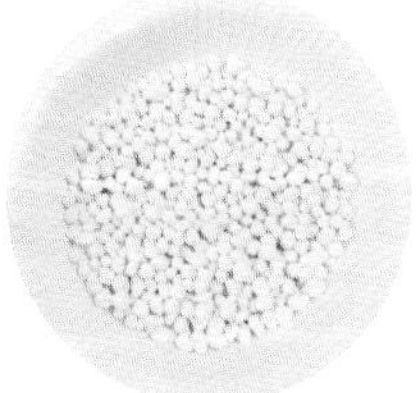

Specific Fertilizer for Hanamono rich in phosphoric acid and potassium
*Make a hole in the soil and bury this type of fertilizer inside it.

4 PROTECTING AGAINST PEST DAMAGE

Growing a bonsai in a good environment (well-ventilated and in good sunlight) suitable for the tree is the very first step in preventing pest damage. Rather than acting after the damage is done, it's best to be proactive and disinfect the bonsai regularly. A good practice is to dilute lime sulfur with water and spray it periodically (usually around once a month) during the winter season (December to March). It is very important to spray the appropriate amount.

The best time of the day and optimal weather for spraying disinfectant depend on the season. Usually, when the temperature is low in the early morning or in the evening, provided that the wind is light, disinfectant should be sprayed on both sides of leaves. Avoid spraying disinfectant when wind is strong or if it's too sunny. In winter, during days of good weather, disinfectant should be sprayed not only on leaves but also on branches and the trunk. Afterward, allow sunlight to hit the tree directly to dry the disinfectant.

◆ AVOIDING ROOT CARCINOMA (ROOT CANCER)

Example: Chojubai

Hanamono are prone to root carcinoma disease. This can be prevented beforehand by disinfecting the bonsai carefully when planting. If you find a diseased root, cut it immediately and burn it to prevent further infection.

1 Submerge the bonsai to the base of the trunk in a basin of water to which fungicide has been added. Allow it to soak for 1–2 hours, then take it out, blot or shake off the water and return the bonsai to the pot. *For fungicide: fill 70/80% of a 2.5 gallon (10 l) bucket with water and add two caps of fungicide.

2 Repeat step **1** but leave the tree inside the pot.

PREPARATION FOR REPLANTING

The first step is to remove the bonsai from its existing pot. New bonsai often come in ceramic pots but young trees can also be sold in simple plastic pots.

Removing a Bonsai from a Ceramic Pot (Example: Tsubaki)

1 A thick wire is wrapped at the bottom of the pot.

2 Cut the center of the wire with pliers.

3 Spread the wire outwards and use the pliers to cut the wire off on both sides.

4 Bottom of the pot with the wire removed.

5 There are two smaller wires; pull them out with the pliers.

6 Loosen the soil around the borders of the pot.

7 Grab the roots with your hands and remove the bonsai from the pot.

8 Carefully loosen the remaining wires.

9 Grasp the wire and remove it with pliers.

Removing a Bonsai from a Plastic Pot (Example: Ezomatsu)

TIP

In the case of plastic pots, the trees are planted deep to make them more stable.

1 Cut the upper part of the plastic pot using pruning shears along with the end of the roots.

2 How it should look once the pot has been "pruned."

3 Pull the plastic pot off (this is how it'll look).

REARRANGING (EXAMPLE: UGUISUKAGURA)

Depending on the tree, bonsai should be repotted every year or two. Trimming a root that has filled its pot has the added benefit of helping the tree retain its size.

1 Reducing the Roots

When cutting the roots with scissors, observe the condition of the roots and choose your cutting method accordingly. Also, in plants such as the Uguisukagura, instead of cutting the roots with scissors, you can scoop away some part of it. In Chapter 3, we will introduce the complete process for each tree species.

When the roots are long
(Example: Ume)

In this case, use rooting scissors to shorten the roots.

When the roots are a bit long
(Example: Sanzashi)

Cut the roots vertically with rooting scissors to loosen.

When the roots are too long
(Example: Ume)

In this case, use rooting scissors to shorten the roots.

When the roots are not long
(Example: Komayumi)

1 Point the roots downwards and carefully untangle them.

MEMO

Plant the bonsai only after you've completely finished wiring the new pot.

Always do wiring before replanting. If wiring is done after replanting, it'll shift the roots and put strain on the bonsai. Also, bonsai become temporarily unstable immediately after replanting, which makes wiring more difficult.

2 Preparing the Pot

➡ See below

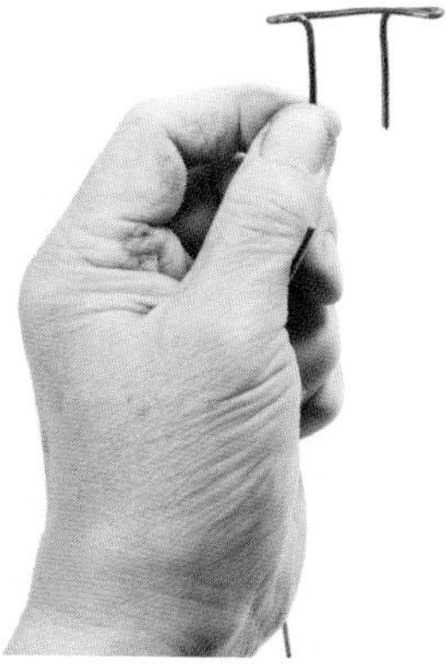

2 Prepare a wire to fix the net to the bottom.

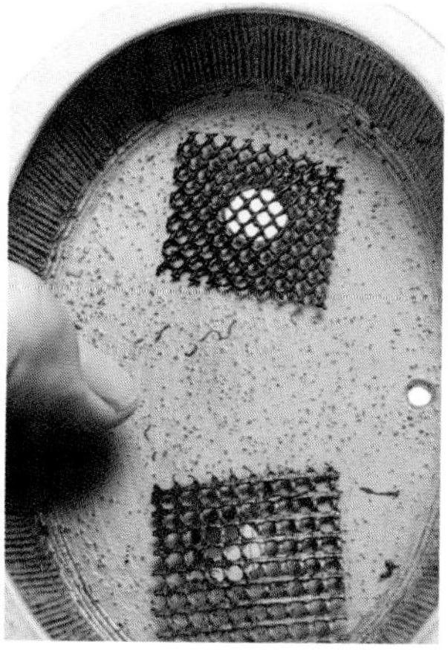

3 Place the net in the bottom of the pot.

4 Pass the wire from step 2 outwards from inside the pot and curl it (as on the upper hole in the photo) and do the same for the other hole as well.

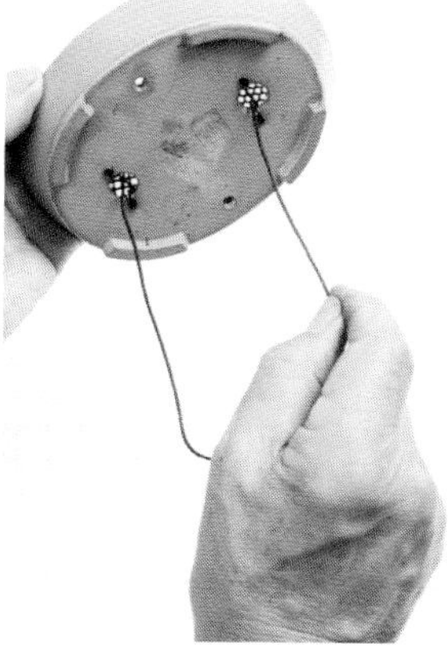

5 From the bottom, pass the wire that will be used to fix the tree through the two holes.

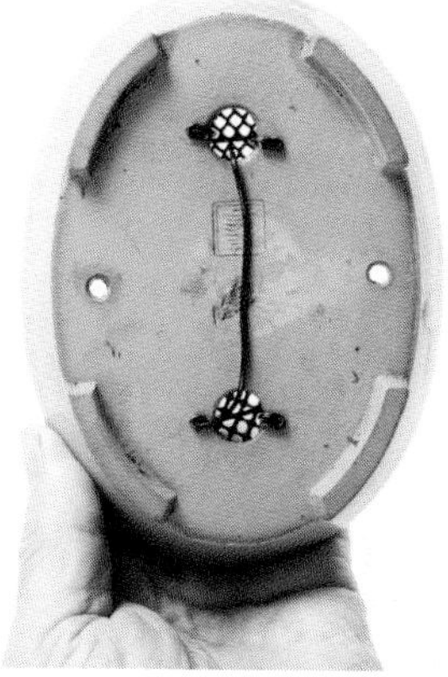

6 Make sure that the wire used for fixing is tight around the bottom of the pot.

7 Place the pot down and spread the wire slightly to the left and right.

MEMO

How to wire the netting to the bottom of the pot

This is tricky at first, but once you're used to it, your hands will move naturally through the process.

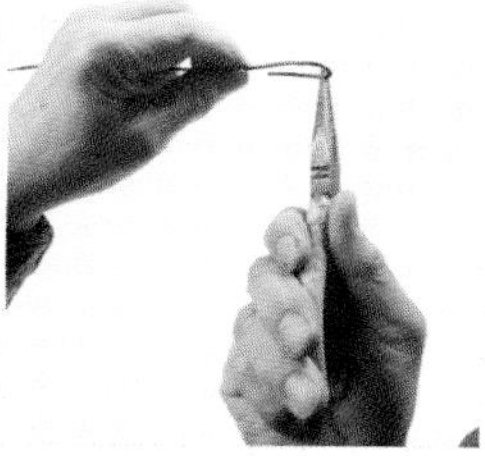

1 Bend the wire with pliers and curl it in a loop.

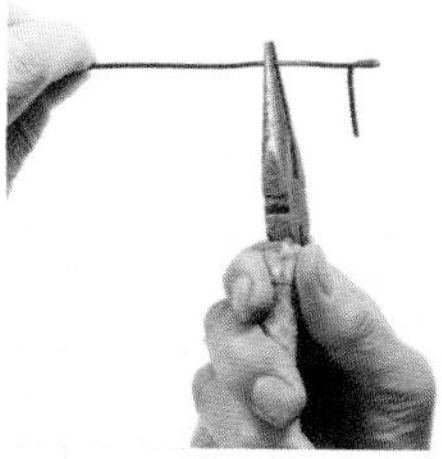

2 Bend the shorter side at a right angle.

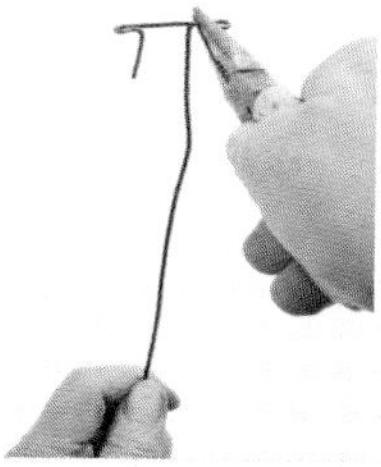

3 Do the same on the opposite side.

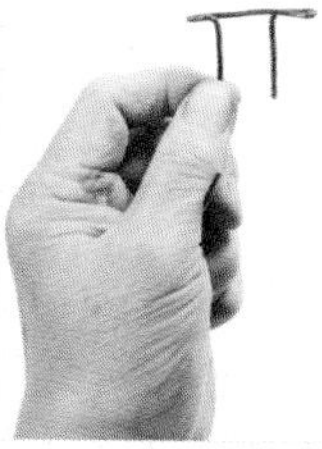

4 Make sure both sides are equal in length. If one side is too long, cut away the excess.

3 Planting the Tree

8 Place the soil in the bottom of the pot.

TIP

The size of the akadama soil used here differs from that used in step 8; the grain on the bottom is usually larger to improve water drainage.

TIP

If you use bamboo charcoal, do not place it on the upper part of the soil since it floats when placed in a bucket of water.

11 Place soil on top as well, and use tweezers to fill the gaps, making sure to leave none.

9 Place the tree in the pot and add more soil around it.

12 After the planting is completed, water with a watering can

10 Place the wire with pliers and fix the tree.

MEMO

Watering from the bottom of the pot

Another way to fully soak the soil is to immerse the just-planted bonsai in a basin of water.

Simple method for fixing trees *(Example: Umedoki)*

If the pot is small and the pot hole is one, this method is easy.

1 Prepare the pot with soil and place the tree inside.

2 Sharpen the tip of the wire with pliers.

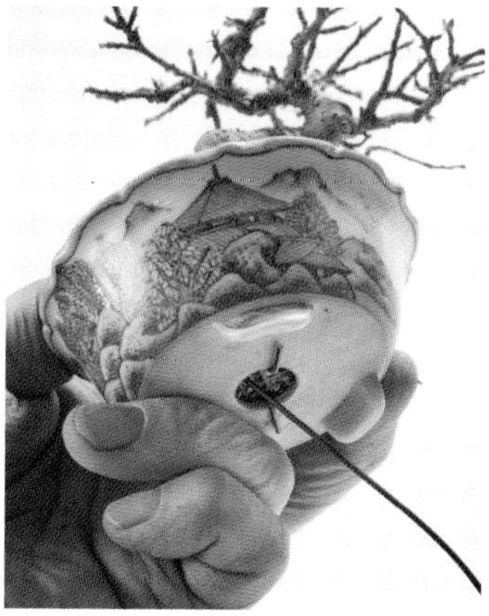

3 Insert the wire from the hole in the bottom of the pot.

4 Pull the wire to the surface of the soil and grasp it with the pliers' tip.

5 Use the pliers' tip to bend the wire in a U shape.

6 Pull the wire as shown, bend it again to fix the tree, and use pliers to cut the extra wire. Repeat on the other side.

ADDING MOSS
(EXAMPLE: SEKKAHINOKI)

Smaller bonsai dry easily. Adding moss will help the bonsai retain more water and will also improve its appearance and value.

Adding/Spreading Moss

TIP

When choosing moss, choose according to the tree's species and environment.

TIP

If thick moss is stretched, it might bend and break after placement, so be careful.

1 Cut the top of the moss small and thin using pruning shears' tips.

2 Grab the moss with the tip of the shears and place it on the soil.

TIP

Spread moss over the whole space and make sure that the moss does not overlap.

3 Lightly hold the moss with your fingers and press onto the soil.

TIP

By spritzing the moss, you are not just cleaning it but also helping it better adapt to the new environment.

4 Sprinkle water on the moss and the pot.

Growing Moss (Example: Zakuro and Keyaki)

If you sprinkle moss with water often, you can grow new moss. For growing moss, early June is ideal.

1 Cut the overgrown moss under the Zakuro using pruning shears.

2 Take the moss from the Zakuro and sprinkle it under the Keyaki.

3 Scatter the moss with tweezers and fill the spaces in between.

4 Lightly press the moss with fingers to flatten it.

TIP

The root of the Zakuro tree was left uncovered to show the spreading of the roots. In the case of other trees, the roots will spread up through the moss.

5 Make sure it's spread uniformly on the soil, except for the root.

MEMO

Tend the freshly laid moss immediately to keep it in place

Freshly laid moss can easily blow away once the bonsai is placed outdoors. Spritz the moss immediately upon spreading to give it weight.

HOW TO COVER THE SOIL, VARIATION

Covering the soil with moss, water moss or sphagnum moss helps prevent the soil from scattering around and dirtying the shelf. At the beginning of the rainy season, the roots will start to stretch, so old moss should be replaced with fresh moss.

Example of Bonsai Combined with Moss

Moss on the surface of the soil is not only effective for water retention; it is also aesthetically pleasing.

Grown moss ➡ p. 38
(Example: Sekkahinoki)

Spread moss ➡ p. 39
(Example: Keyaki)

Example of Bonsai Combined with Water Moss

It is elegant to spread moss on top of water moss. Also, if you put a net over the water moss, it'll keep the soil safe from heavy rain or heavy wind.

Water moss spread in a string shape ➡ p. 208
(Example: Karin)

Spread moss over water moss ➡ p. 137
(Example: Himeshara)

Net placed over the water moss ➡ p. 224
(Example: Tachibana Modoki)

WIRING THE BRANCHES
(EXAMPLE: TSUBAKI)

For branch wiring we start from the lower branches. The thickness of the wire depends on the thickness of the branch. Wiring should go all the way to the tip of the branch.

1 Place the center of the wire on the branch.

2 Fix the wire by entwining it in the second branch (branch in front).

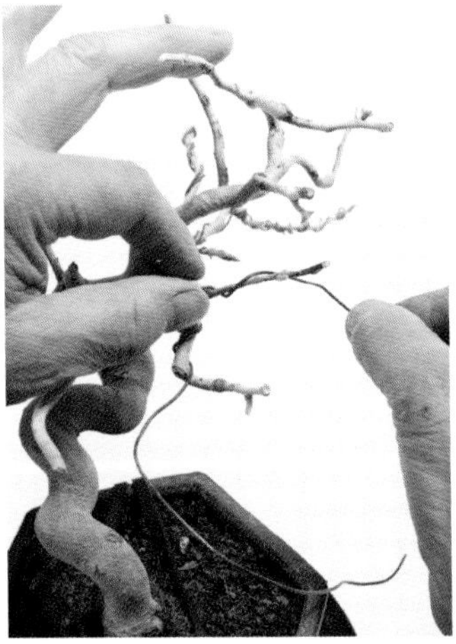

3 Fix the wire on the first branch (branch in back).

4 Once the first branch (branch in the back) is covered, cut the excess with pliers.

5 Repeat for the second branch (branch in front).

6 Once done, it should look like this.

WIRING Q & A

Q: How do I choose the thickness of the wire?

A: It should be chosen according to the thickness of the branch. If you are a beginner, you'll mostly deal with young trees, so the most common thickness will be 1–2 mm.

Q: How do I choose the type of wire?

A: For wiring, the most commonly used are copper or aluminum. Copper wire is harder to handle but is more camouflaged, making the tree more elegant. On the other hand, aluminum wire is softer and easier to use but it's easily spotted and not very elegant.

Q: How tight should the wiring be?

A: It is important not to wrap the wire so tightly that it interferes with the tree's condition, but it should also not be too loose. There is no specific rule for this, but it's important to keep a certain balance.

Q: How do I take off the wire?

A: Cut the wire piece by piece with cutters, starting from the upper branches. The best way to do it is to make one cut per roll around the branch.

Q: When should the wire be removed?

A: You can remove the wire when the desired shape is achieved, or you can leave it on if it's not damaging the tree. It's best to remove the wire before pruning the shaped bonsai.

TIP

When you're ready to remove wire from a new tree, try to get a demo from an expert. Observing is the best way to learn this process.

TAKING CARE OF THE TREE

After repotting and wiring, you need to take care of the bonsai according to the season. Check on the state of your tree and act accordingly.

Sprout Plucking

If you catch them before they grow, you can pluck them out with tweezers.

Momiji

Sprout Cutting

If they grow long, cut the longest ones with scissors.

Karin

Leaf Cutting

Before they grow, you can pluck them out with tweezers.

Tachibana Modoki

TIP

There are three main benefits of leaf cutting. ① It results in superior fall colors ② It increases the tree's ramification—two years' worth can be achieved in a single year. ③ As the cutting nears completion, it allows more light and air to reach previously shaded areas.

Arranging

Cut the lower leaves using pruning scissors and clean the periphery of the trunk.

Kuromatsu

Pruning (before)

Cut off branches that are bad (see next page) or spoil the shape of the tree using pruning scissors and arrange the branches.

Ichii

Pruning (after)

After pruning, the tree is approaching the ideal shape.

MEMO

How to pollinate

1. It's possible that ants will carry pollen to the nectar of female flowers.
2. As shown in the photo, there are ways to directly pollinate male and female trees.
3. Just by placing a male tree next to a female, pollination occurs thanks to wind.

Mayumi

WHEN PRUNING, CUT THE BAD BRANCHES

1 Long branches

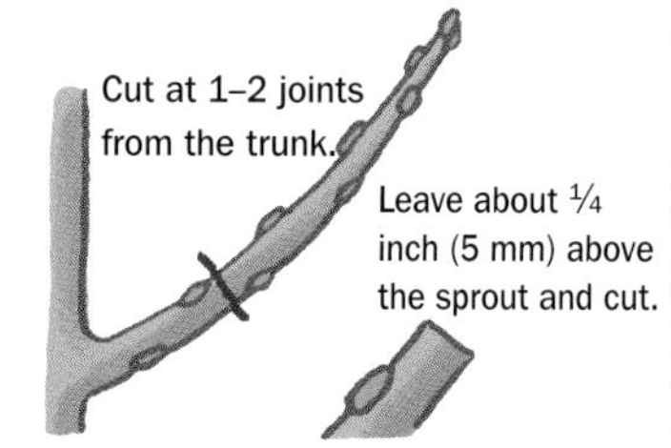

2 Standing branches

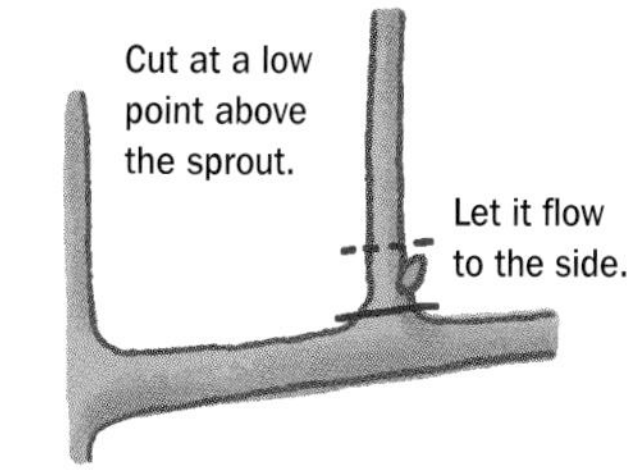

3 Hanging branches

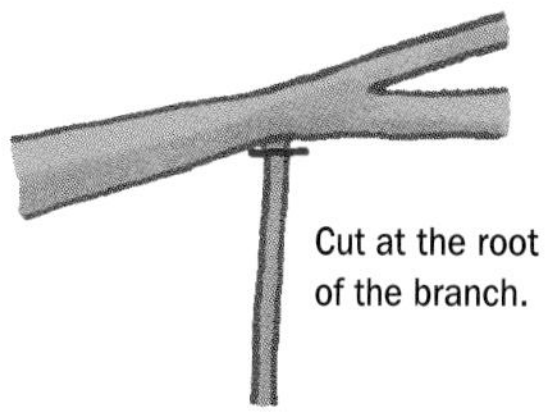

4 Parallel branches

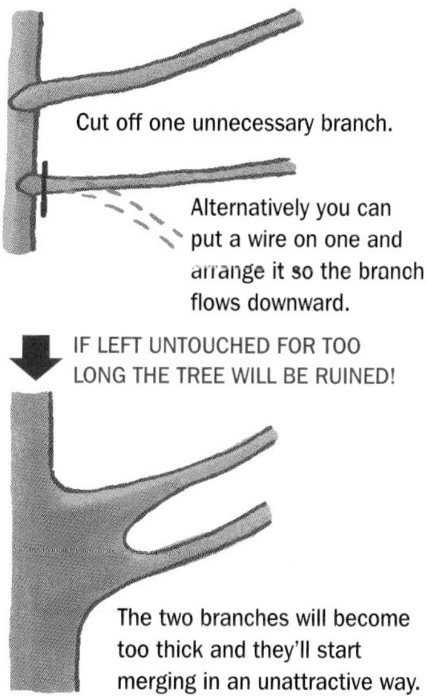

5 Bar-shaped branches

If there are two branches coming from two different sides but at the same height.

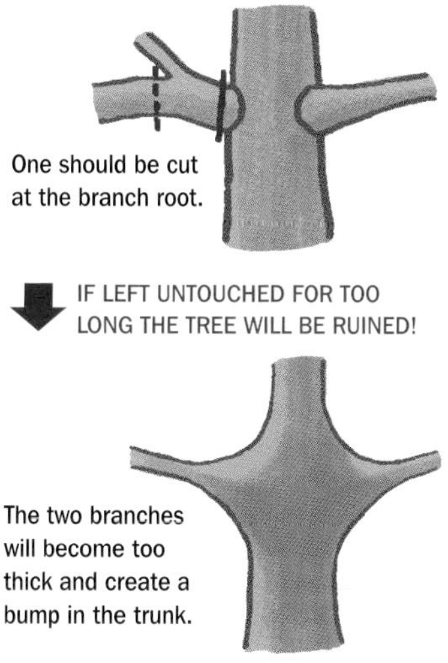

6 Wheel branches

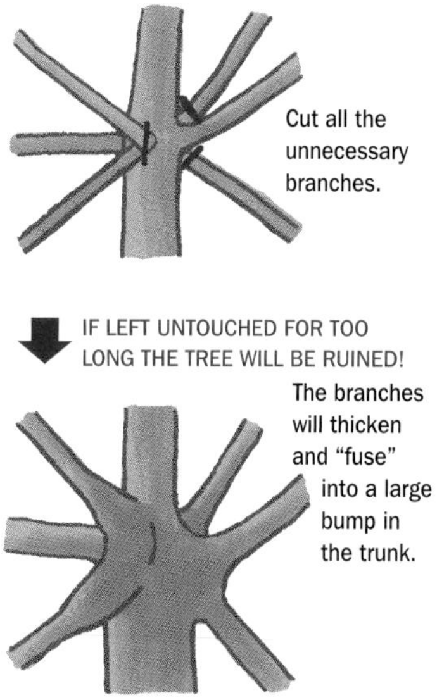

7 Intersecting branches

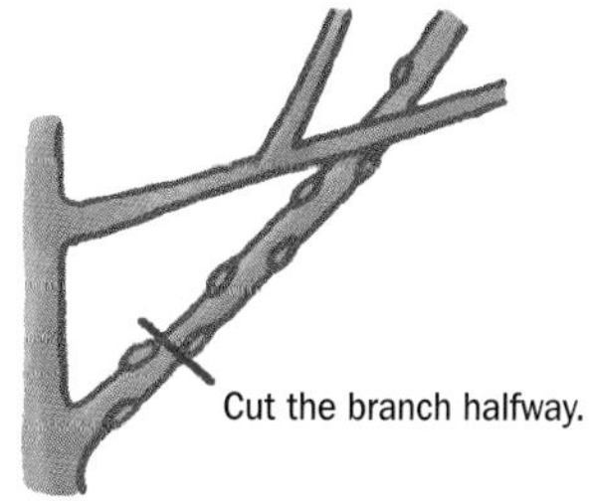

8 Overlapping branches

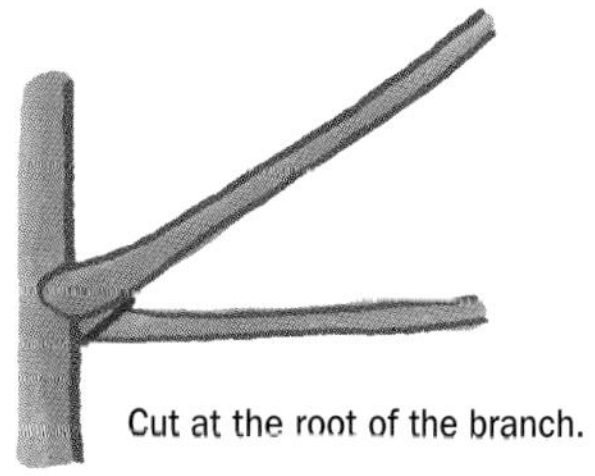

9 Inverted branches

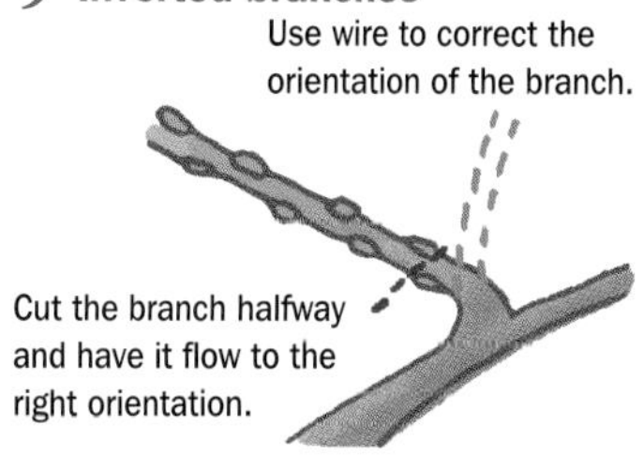

10 Thick branches

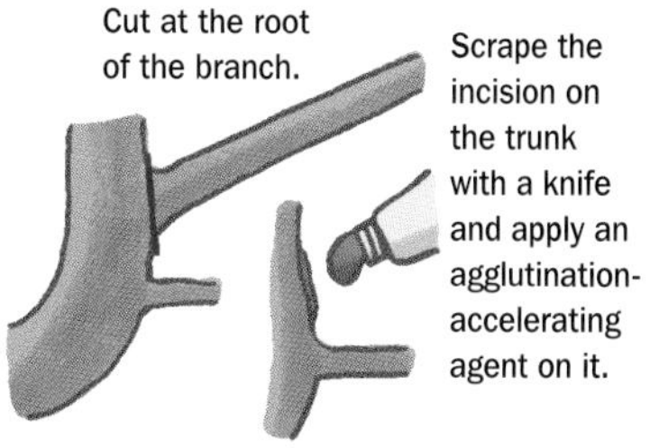

11 Inside branches

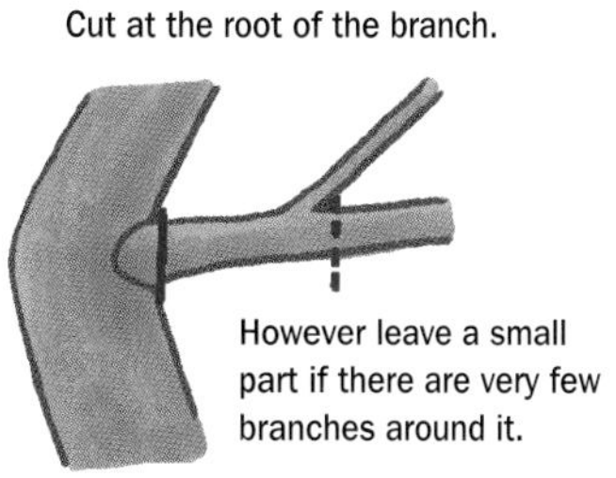

12 "Frog" branches

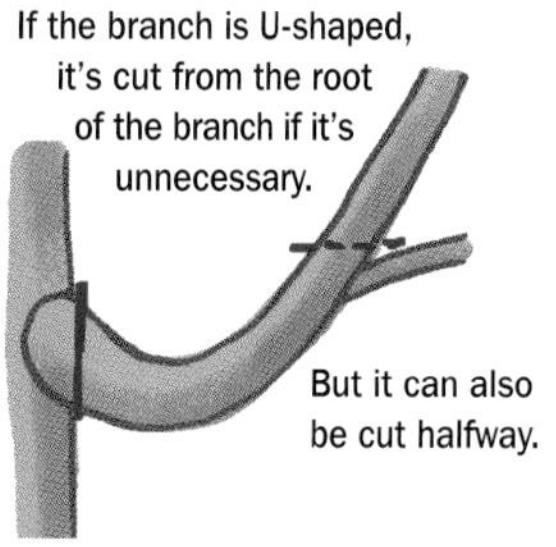

CREATING JIN OR SHARI (EXAMPLE: SHINPAKU)

Cutting the trunk and branches will make trees look aged and exposed to wind or snow. Once you learn the trick to it, even beginners can do it easily.

Jin

1 Cut unnecessary branches.

2 Strip the branches with a knife.

3 This is how the stripped branch should look.

4 Tear off the stripped branch with split scissors and let the Jin (branch) break in a way that looks natural.

5 The Jin is now complete!

Shari

1 Scrape the trunk with a router to make a Shari (trunk).

TIP

If you do not leave the brown part (that's still alive) intact, the branch will wither, so be careful.

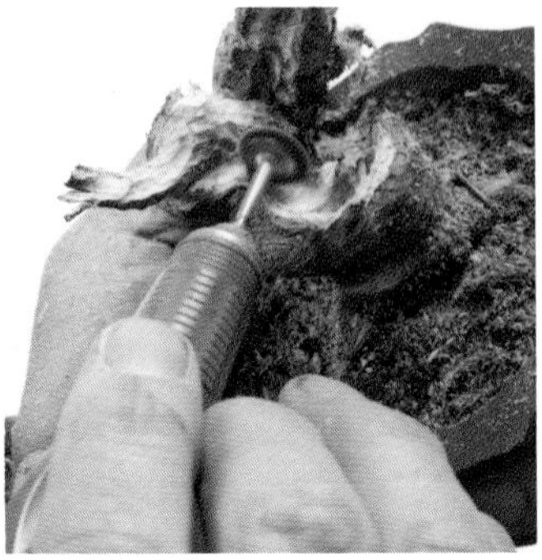

2 Brush the scraped trunk with a wire brush.

3 The Shari is now complete.

Protecting the Jin and Shari

1 One month after creating the Jin or Shari, dilute the lime sulfur agent and brush it on the Jin or Shari with a soft brush.

TIP

You can also make the Jin and Shari white.

2 Three or four months later, repeat the process. This is how it should look the day after brushing the tree.

TIP

After this, in a few months, moss will try to grow on Jin or Shari. In that case, wash it with a brush and dry it, then reapply the lime sulfur agent. Apply the agent twice a year.

Protecting the old parts of Jin and Shari with rosin

As they grow older, the Jin and Shari tend to grow fat. If you add grease/oil to the resin, it will repel water and have an antiseptic effect. Also, instead of brushing the rosin as is, dissolve it in anhydrous ethanol so it will permeate better.

1 Put the rosin (solid) into anhydrous ethanol (liquid) and dissolve.

Protect only the old (dark) part of the trunk, as it's useless on the younger part.

TIP

Applying protection to the young part is unnecessary and wasteful.

2 Using a syringe or brush, evenly apply the solution from step **1**.

TIP

After applying your solution, clean your syringe. Brush it with ethanol to prevent hardening.

IMPROVING/INCREASING YOUR BONSAI

Here we introduce basic bonsai methods such as root splitting, planting, layering and yobitsugi. Since growing fruits from seeds takes a long time, it is not recommended for beginners.

Root splitting

Layering

Planting

Yobitsugi

After purchasing young trees and growing your bonsai through time and effort, you'll gradually get attached to it, and it will truly become your own. At that point, you'll feel attached even to the unnecessary branches you remove from your tree. Fortunately, there's a use for them. If, for example, you cut branches and "plant" them, you can grow up to three or four branches. And if the pot becomes completely full, you can "split the roots" in two separate pots.

When the trunk grows too long and the tree starts losing shape, you "layer" the tree, making the trunk shorter while at the same time shifting the bonsai into a new shape. And, if you want a new branch from the trunk, you can use the yobitsugi to create one. Bonsai are living creatures, so we can keep breeding new trees and keep aiming at the ideal tree shape.

Root Splitting (Example: Yamaajisai)

Mid-June: We split one bonsai into two.

1 State when removed from the pot.

2 Scrape the roots downwards.

3 State of the roots after scraping.

4 Cut the root in the middle using rooting scissors.

5 Pull the two sides with your hands, separating the plant into two.

6 Rearrange the tree from step **5** into a new pot.

Cutting and Planting (Example: Chirimenkazura)

First part of April—Take a branch from a parent tree during pruning and cultivate with soil and water.

Parent Tree

1 Prune unnecessary thick branches.

2 Take a branch from step 1 to plant and carve the end where the branch was cut with a knife.

TIP

Carving with scissors or similar will damage the trunk's fiber. Use a sharp knife to carve the end.

Child Tree

3 These are the branches we took from the parent tree.

4 Put the soil into the new pot, take the branches from step 3 and push them into the soil with tweezers.

※Use akadama soil, medium size.

5 State of the branches once they are planted in the new pot.

TIP

When pruning a thick branch, protect the incision on the parent tree by applying a healing coating agent.

MEMO

Management after planting

Place a saucer under the pot, and pour water. Place the pot in a spot that's neither too bright nor too dark and protect it with a wire cover. It will take about 2–3 months for the roots to grow out from the bottom.

Child Tree (One year later)

6 State of the branch from step **5** after one year, once removed from soil.

9 Prepare the pots and replant (akadama medium grain).

7 Cut the upper root away from the rest.

10 If the roots are not firm, fix them with wire.

8 State of the branch after step **7**.

11 Final state of the new bonsai.

Layering (Example: Sakura)

First half of March—The period before the leaves/flowers of the cherry blossom appear is a suitable time for layering.

1 Lock the binding band around the trunk and choose the position for the layering.

2 Use a saw to cut the bark around the circumference at the top and the bottom of the binding band.

3 Peel off the bark.

4 State of the tree after the bark has been peeled off.

5 In order to encourage the growth of a new branch, only the upper side should be carved a little bit deeper.

6 Apply a rooting agent only to the upper part.

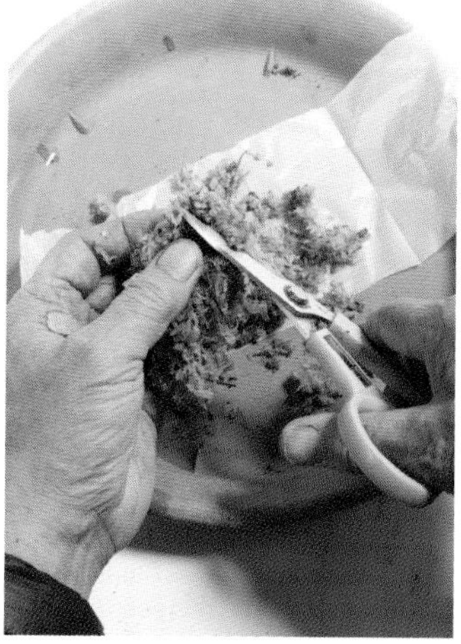

7 Soak water moss in some water, squeeze, and cut it to the size of about ⅜ in (1 cm) using rooting scissors.

8 Place the moss flat on stretched plastic and hold it against the area we cut.

TIP

The reason we cut the moss and make it smaller is to ensure that the new roots won't get stuck when growing.

9 Wrap the plastic around the trunk over the cut area.

10 Wrap a wire downwards to fix it in place.

11 By mid June, the bonsai should look like this.

MEMO

Rules after layering

After the layering is completed, place the pot in partial shade. Water the entire tree, especially from above the moss. Around June, the new root should have already started branching out of the plastic. However, leave the plastic wrapped around until the next spring and wait until the new root has grown thicker and stronger. When the root is hard enough, cut it with a root saw, remove the plastic, and plant it in soil.

Yobitsugi (Example: Yama momiji)

First half of June—When you want a new branch in a certain position, you can achieve this by transplanting other branches. This is yobitsugi.

TIP

In the case of bonsai, each branch is named according to its position as seen from above the pot: furthest right is "branch 1," next is "branch 2" and so on.

1 Since the tree's form is poor, we'll call the branch on the far right "branch 1" and graft it.

2 We want a branch growing from this position (indicated by the tweezers).

3 Entwine the graft branch (branch rightmost from step **1**).

TIP

Bring the branch around to where the graft will be applied and turn the trunk.

4 Bend and bring the graft branch to the point where we want the new branch.

5 Peel off the outer skin of the branch with a scalpel.

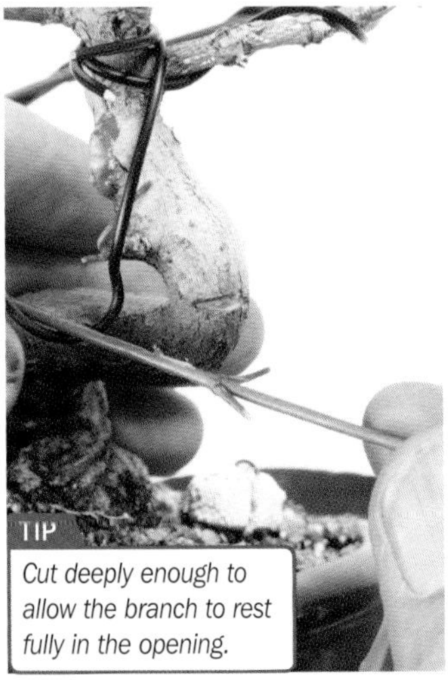

TIP

Cut deeply enough to allow the branch to rest fully in the opening.

6 Carve the trunk's bark with the scalpel as well.

7 Wrap with grafting tape and pull the two wounds close.

8 Place wire around it so that it lightly pushes them together.

9 Cut the excess wire.

10 Wire one branch at a time.

11 State of the tree after “branch 1” grafting is completed.

MEMO

When to remove the wire and grafting tape

Usually it takes 2–3 months for grafting to complete. You can perform yobitsugi on any species. For evergreens, grafting takes up to three years to complete.

column 2

Pointers on Selecting Bonsai

As with any plant, when choosing a bonsai, the most important thing is to select a healthy tree. No matter how beautiful its shape, always avoid the ones that are weak, diseased or withering. Since we will be caring for our bonsai for many years, it makes sense to be cautious when choosing this lifelong companion.

It may be difficult for beginners to know how to examine a bonsai. Ask your vendor any and every question that comes to mind. Withered leaves or peeling bark may be natural for the tree at a given time of year and not related to illness or damage. It's important to ask.

Also, when looking at young trees, it's very hard for beginners to envisage what it will look like in the future. A good vendor will be experienced, rather like a sculptor who looks at stone and can already see the finished work carved out of the material. Talk with your vendor about your bonsai until you feel well informed.

The most important consideration when choosing a young bonsai is your own affinity. If a tree makes you think, "This could be really lovely" as you're observing it, that could be the start of a beautiful friendship.

CHAPTER 3

BONSAI ACCORDING TO PLANT CATEGORY

PRESENTATION OF THE BONSAI We will introduce the basics of the bonsai and its origin, highlights and tips for raising it.

ITEMS REQUIRED AND TIMING The timing for each process will be explained.

APPRECIATING THE BONSAI We will introduce a model bonsai, usually placed on a table or baseboard.

PROFILE We will introduce aliases and the family of the specific tree.

PROCESS We will explain every step of each process, so that even beginners can be successful at making wonderful bonsai.

BONSAI'S NAME In Romaji and Kanji.

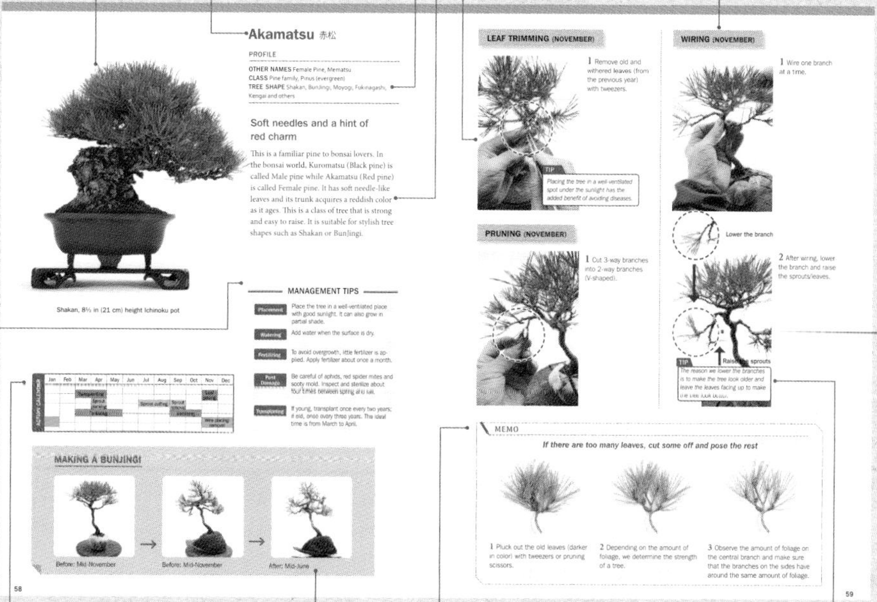

MANAGEMENT TIPS Important information about growing the bonsai, such as correct placement and best watering method.

ACTION CALENDAR These cover all the steps to be performed over the course of a year.

CHANGES FROM BEFORE AND AFTER ARTIFICIAL PROCESSES Photos to help you see the changes the bonsai goes through at various times.

MEMO These explain more advanced techniques and provide additional information.

TIP Additional helpful info in a concise format.

RED CIRCLES Red circles direct your attention to specific points.

Akamatsu 赤松

Shakan, 8½ in (21 cm) height Ichinoku pot

PROFILE

OTHER NAMES Female Pine, Mematsu
CLASS Pine family, Pinus (evergreen)
TREE SHAPE Shakan, BunJingi, Moyogi, Fukinagashi, Kengai and others

Soft needles and a hint of red charm

This is a familiar pine to bonsai lovers. In the bonsai world, Kuromatsu (Black pine) is called Male pine while Akamatsu (Red pine) is called Female pine. It has soft needle-like leaves and its trunk acquires a reddish color as it ages. This is a class of tree that is strong and easy to raise. It is suitable for stylish tree shapes such as Shakan or BunJingi.

ACTION CALENDAR	Jan	Feb	Mar	Apr	May	Jun	Jul	Aug	Sep	Oct	Nov	Dec
			Transplanting								Leaf posing	
				Sprout plucking			Sprout cutting		Sprout removal			
			Fertilizing						Fertilizing			
											Wire placing/ removal	

MANAGEMENT TIPS

Placement Place the tree in a well-ventilated place with good sunlight. It can also grow in partial shade.

Watering Add water when the surface is dry.

Fertilizing To avoid overgrowth, little fertilizer is applied. Apply fertilizer about once a month.

Pest Damage Be careful of aphids, red spider mites and sooty mold. Inspect and sterilize about four times between spring and fall.

Transplanting If young, transplant once every two years; if old, once every three years. The ideal time is from March to April.

MAKING A BUNJINGI

Before: Mid-November

→

Before: Mid-November

→

After: Mid-June

LEAF TRIMMING (NOVEMBER)

1 Remove old and withered leaves (from the previous year) with tweezers.

TIP

Placing the tree in a well-ventilated spot under the sunlight has the added benefit of avoiding diseases.

PRUNING (NOVEMBER)

1 Cut 3-way branches into 2-way branches (V-shaped).

WIRING (NOVEMBER)

1 Wire one branch at a time.

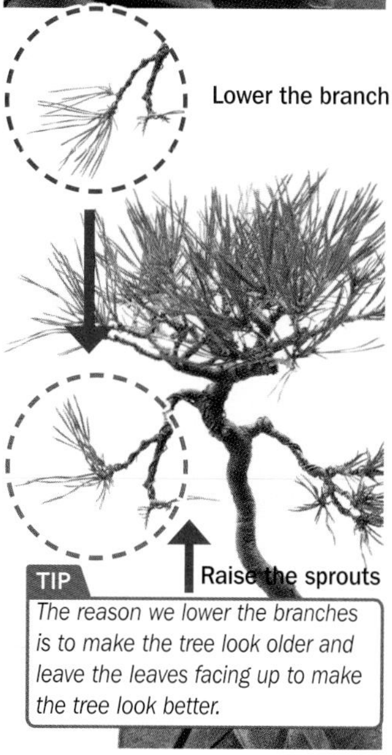

2 After wiring, lower the branch and raise the sprouts/leaves.

TIP

The reason we lower the branches is to make the tree look older and leave the leaves facing up to make the tree look better.

MEMO

If there are too many leaves, cut some off and pose the rest

1 Pluck out the old leaves (darker in color) with tweezers or pruning scissors.

2 Depending on the amount of foliage, we determine the strength of a tree.

3 Observe the amount of foliage on the central branch and make sure that the branches on the sides have around the same amount of foliage.

PRUNING (NOVEMBER)

1 Cut ⅓ of the length of the leaves.

2 Cut long roots using rooting scissors.

TRANSPLANTING (NOVEMBER)

TIP

Depending on the Matsu's sap, the roots may have turned rock solid.

TIP

Transplanting in March–April may work out, but the roots will not come apart.

1 Scoop the soil away vertically with a rake.

3 Place the tree on artificial carved stones (kurama stones), roll up keto soil and spread it around the roots.

MEMO

Removing the Hakama

The Hakama is the portion at the base of each branch that looks like fish scales. It can be removed with tweezers. Doing this gives the branches a clean look and can also prevent dirt or mold from growing on the branches.

4 Spritz to moisturize.

TIP

After spritzing, the soil will become softer, and it becomes easier to spread moss.

5 Appearance after the transplanting is completed and moss has been spread.

SPROUT CUTTING (MID-JUNE)

1 Appearance of grown sprouts.

2 Cut the sprouts at base.

TIP

If the sprouts are cut too late, they won't regrow much. On the other hand, if they're cut too early, they may overgrow and cause problems.

3 Appearance after the sprout cutting is completed.

MEMO

Ways to prune Matsu the "Short Leaves" way

Bud Picking = Prune the buds that grew out in April by pinching the ends with your fingers.

Bud Trimming = From May to July, trim the buds from the base to encourage the second buds to grow out.

Bud Walling = In mid-September, the second buds will have grown out. Trim or pick out the excess buds.

Ichii 一位

PROFILE

OTHER NAMES Onko, Araragi, water pine (Mizumatsu)
CLASS Taxaceae (evergreen tall tree)
TREE SHAPE Chokkan, Shakan, Moyogi, Kabutachi and others

Kabutachi, 6¼–6¾ in (16–17 cm) height, on rock

An easy tree to grow, with dense, glossy leaves

This strong tree grows everywhere in Japan. Since the trunk is very resistant to decay, when used as lumber, it was called Ichii (Number One/The Best). The tree buds frequently, so the leaves are very dense and tree shapes are very easy to create with this species. Unusual among evergreens, Ichii is usually grown in shade or partial shade.

ACTION CALENDAR

Jan	Feb	Mar	Apr	May	Jun	Jul	Aug	Sep	Oct	Nov	Dec
		Transplanting									
				Sprout plucking							
				Fertilizing					Fertilizing		
	Wire placing/ removal										

MANAGEMENT TIPS

Placement Shade or partial shade. Avoid direct sunlight, especially during summer, but keep it in a well-ventilated spot.

Watering It loves water (hence the nickname "water pine") so be careful not to let it dry out.

Fertilizing To keep the color of the leaves glossy, use plenty of fertilizer. Give solid fertilizer once a month.

Pest Damage Be careful of scale insects, moths and mold.

Transplanting If it's young, do this once every two years; if old, once every three years. The best time is between March and April.

MAKING A HANKENGAI

Before: Late April

→

After: Late April

PRUNING (LATE APRIL)

1 Cut the thick branches with branch-cutting scissors.

TIP

Since the thick branches are straight and cannot be bent even with wire, we keep only the branches that are easier to arrange in our desired shape.

2 Appearance after cutting one thick branch.

TIP

We do not apply any agent to the incision this time. When the incision gets older, we will make a Jin out of it.

3 Appearance after all thick branches are cut.

4 Long branches are also cut using pruning scissors.

5 Appearance after the long branches are cut.

WIRING (LATE APRIL)

1 Wrap one branch at a time and arrange the branches.

2 Appearance after the wiring is completed.

TRANSPLANTING (LATE APRIL)

1 Cut the roots vertically using rooting scissors.

2 Scoop the soil away downwards with a rake.

3 Cut long roots using rooting scissors.

4 Appearance of the roots after the cutting is completed.

5 Prepare the pot and the lower soil (80% akadama medium grain; 20% river sand).

※Use a mixture of 80% akadama medium grain, 20% river sand.

6 Fix the wire in one place with pliers, turn the wire on the back side and fix the tree.

※Use a mixture of 80% akadama small grain, 20% river sand.

7 Place the top layer of soil (80% akadama small grain; 20% river sand) from the top.

8 Appearance after transplanting is completed and moss is spread.

SPROUT PLUCKING (EARLY JUNE)

1 Hold the base of the sprouts and pluck them out with tweezers.

2 Also pluck out the old leaves (darker in color) in the same way.

Ezomatsu 蝦夷松

PROFILE

OTHER NAMES Aka ezomatsu (shikotanmatsu)
CLASS Picea jezoensis (evergreen)
TREE SHAPE Chokkan, Shakan, Moyogi, Ishitsuki and others

Shakan, 6¼ in (16 cm) height, Ishitsuki (on stone)

The nature of Japan's northern regions is depicted through this tree

This type of tree grows only in the difficult sort of weather typical of northern Japan (Hokkaido). Yatsubusa (dwarf bonsai) creation is easy to do with this species. Since the spring buds are bright green, they create a beautiful tree. This tree can cling to a rock (ishitsuki), giving it a natural atmosphere. The branches can easily grow disorganized, making the tree look older. You can also create Shari with this tree.

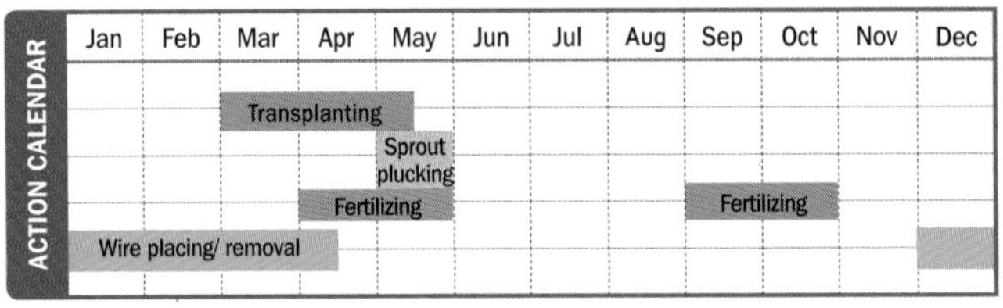

MANAGEMENT TIPS

Placement Under sunlight and in a well-ventilated spot. In summer, partial shade is enough; in winter, move it under an overhang or similar.

Watering It dries rather quickly, so water it often. Make sure it doesn't dry up during summer. During summer also spritz the leaves with water.

Fertilizing Once a month, hard type.

Pest Damage Be careful of spider mites; these can be prevented by spritzing the leaves.

Transplanting If it's young, do this once every two years; if old, once every three years. The best time is between March and mid-May.

MAKING A HIRAISHI

Before: Mid-April

→

After: Mid-May

PREPARATION FOR TRANSPLANTING (MID-APRIL)

1 Cut the upper part of the plastic pot and remove it, along with the excess root, using pruning scissors.

TIP

For seeding pots, if you press the plant in deeply, the plant will be set in place.

2 Appearance after step **1**.

TIP

After removing the roots, we decide on the tree shape.

PRUNING (MID-APRIL)

1 Prune branches that are overcrowded with leaves, using pruning scissors.

TIP

By leaving the branches clear, the leaves will grow denser. Having small but plentiful sprouts is how we can achieve a Yatsubusa.

WIRING/BRANCH ARRANGING (MID-APRIL)

1 Wrap one branch at a time and arrange them.

2 Appearance after wiring is completed.

SPROUT PLUCKING (MID-MAY)

1 Appearance when sprouts are overgrown.

2 Pluck the sprouts by pulling downward with tweezers.

TRANSPLANTING (MID-MAY)

1 Appearance after removing the plastic pot.

2 Prepare the pot.

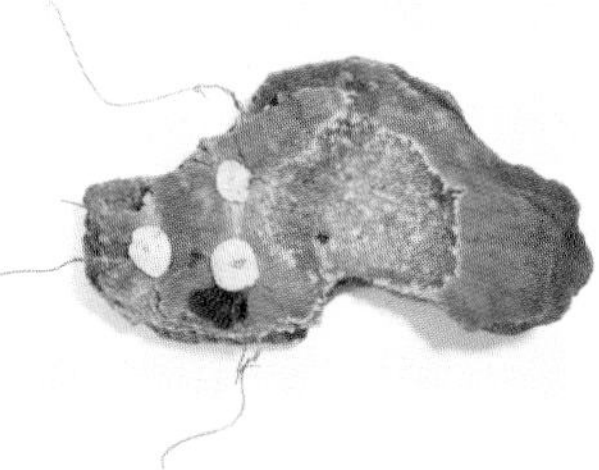

> **TIP**
> *We chose an elegant Hiraishi stone as the pot. Water pools on the right side.*

3 Choose the placement for the tree on the stone.

4 Place keto soil on the spot chosen in step **3**.

5 Hold the roots steadily with your fingers and fix the tree.

6 Use wire in three spots to fix the tree, bend the wire with pliers and cut the excess with scissors.

7 Spread lumps of keto soil around the roots and shape it.

8 Appearance after spreading the keto soil.

9 Plant several Satsuki roots (also known as Saotome) around the soil and spread moss.

10 Appearance after planting Satsuki and spreading moss.

Kuromatsu 黒松

PROFILE

OTHER NAMES Omatsu, male pine
CLASS Pine family, Pinus (evergreen)
TREE SHAPE Chokkan, Shakan, Soukan, BunJingi, Moyogi, Kengai and others

Shakan, 7½ in (19 cm) height, vermilion pot

Straight, hard needle-like leaves and a strong, rough bark

Pines have an important role in making Japan what it is today. Usually, the very first tree people associate with bonsai is the extremely popular Kuromatsu, which is said to be the "male" pine. It's recommended for beginners because it's robust and easy to raise.

ACTION CALENDAR

Jan	Feb	Mar	Apr	May	Jun	Jul	Aug	Sep	Oct	Nov	Dec
		Transplanting	Transplanting							Leaf posing	
			Sprout plucking		Sprout cutting	Sprout cutting		Sprout removal			
		Fertilizing	Fertilizing	Fertilizing				Fertilizing	Fertilizing		
Wire placing/ removal	Wire placing/ removal	Wire placing/ removal									

MANAGEMENT TIPS

Placement Place in a well-ventilated and well-lit place. It can also be raised in partial shade.

Watering Whenever the surface of the soil is dry, give plenty of water.

Fertilizing Place plenty of solid-type fertilizers.

Pest Damage Be careful about aphids, spider mites and leaf-withering diseases. Sprinkle the tree with insecticide.

Transplanting If it's young do this once every two years, old once every three years. The best time is between March and April.

MAKING A SHAKAN

Before: Mid-November

→

After: Early April

→

After: Mid-June

SPROUT PRUNING (MID-NOVEMBER)

1 Cut the lower sprouts using pruning scissors.

PRUNING (MID-NOVEMBER)

1 Cut the thick straight main trunk using pruning shears.

2 Appearance after the main trunk has been cut.

3 Cut the leaves at the base using pruning scissors and make sure the quantity of leaves is balanced on the entire tree.

4 Appearance after the leaf quantity has been balanced out.

5 Apply a coating agent on the wound made by cutting the main trunk.

6 "Average up" the length of all leaves.

WIRING/BRANCH ARRANGING (MID-NOVEMBER)

1 Wrap one branch at a time and arrange them.

2 Appearance after wiring is completed.

TRANSPLANTING (EARLY APRIL)

1 Scoop the soil away downwards with a rake.

TIP

The Kuromatsu was planted in sand, so it is easily removed.

2 Appearance after scooping is finished.

3 Cut and remove the wire that held the tree, using pruning scissors.

4 Cut the long roots, this is the appearance after the roots are cut.

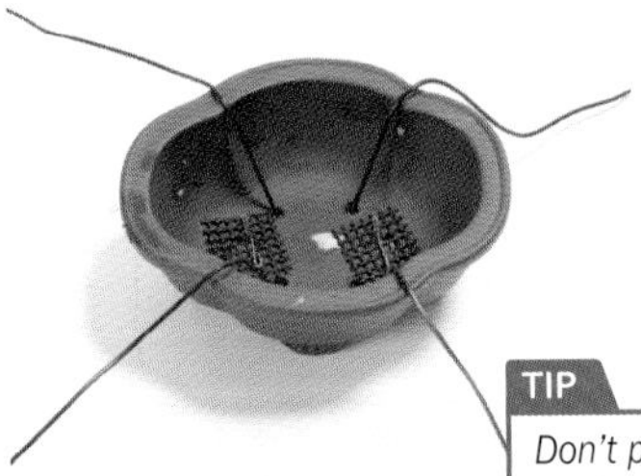

5 Prepare the pot and add the soil (akadama medium grain 70%, river sand 30%; add around 10% bamboo charcoal and mix together).

TIP

Don't place the bamboo charcoal on the surface of the soil; it will float if you immerse the pot in water.

6 Appearance after the transplanting is completed, with moss spread on the soil.

SPROUT CUTTING (MID-JUNE)

1 Appearance of overgrown new sprouts.

2 Take the sprouts that bud this year and shorten them (don't cut at the base).

TIP

If you cut the sprouts at their root, the sap will come out and ruin the sprouts.

3 Appearance after the sprout cutting is completed.

MEMO

Details to keep in mind during sprout cutting

1 **Young sprouts**
Do not cut the youngest buds.

2 **Watering**
Do not water the day before cutting the sprouts. If the soil is dry, it won't produce much sap, reducing the chances of ruining the sprouts. After cutting, however, give plenty of water.

3 **Fertilizing**
After cutting, don't fertilize, so as to avoid overgrowing the leaves again before the time is right. Start giving plenty of fertilizer again in mid-September to strengthen the tree.

Goyoumatsu 五葉松

Shakan, 8 in (20 cm) height, vermilion mortar pot

PROFILE

OTHER NAMES Himekomatsu
CLASS Pine family, Pinus (evergreen)
TREE SHAPE Chokkan, Shakan, Moyogi, BunJingi, Kengai and others

Representing bonsai with dignity and style

This tree grows in the rocky areas on tall mountains throughout all of Japan. From each leaf, five leaves emerge. Having shorter leaves, they naturally shed during the fall, so they are less time-consuming. It takes a long time to grow and start taking on a look of antiquity, but it is possible to make Jin and Shari.

ACTION CALENDAR

Jan	Feb	Mar	Apr	May	Jun	Jul	Aug	Sep	Oct	Nov	Dec
							Transplanting			Leaf posing	
			Sprout plucking								
			Fertilizing						Fertilizing		
Wire placing/ removal									Wire placing/ removal		

MANAGEMENT TIPS

Placement Place in a well-ventilated and well-lit spot. It can also be raised in partial shade.

Watering Moderate the amount of water during spring/summer, so that leaves won't grow too long.

Fertilizing Give solid fertilizer. Fertilize moderately during spring to avoid leaves growing too long.

Pest Damage Be careful about aphids and leaf-withering diseases. Sprinkle the tree with insecticide.

Transplanting If it's young, do this once every two years; if old, once every three years. The best time is between March and April or between August and September.

MAKING A SHAKAN

Before: Mid-November

→

After: Early April

PRUNING (MID-NOVEMBER)

1 Cut the old leaves (from the previous year) using pruning shears.

TIP

Doing this will slow down the tree's growth rate.

2 Cut the center and uppermost branch using pruning shears.

3 Cut the leaves at base using pruning scissors and make sure that the quantity of leaves is balanced on the entire tree.

4 Also shorten the excess branches using pruning scissors, but don't cut them at their base.

TIP

When cutting at the very base of the branch, the sap will seep out and the trunk will turn white and be very difficult to remove later on. Give it a year before cutting the branches' base.

5 Appearance after shortening a branch.

WIRING (MID-NOVEMBER)

1 Wrap one branch at a time and arrange them.

2 After wiring, lower the branches and point the sprouts upwards.

TIP

To give the plant a retro look, point the branches downward and the leaves upward.

3 Cut the unnecessary branches using pruning shears.

4 Appearance after the wiring is completed.

TRANSPLANTING (EARLY APRIL)

1 Remove the pot.

TIP

The white substance around the roots is symbiotic bacteria, an indicator that the tree is growing healthy.

2 Cut the roots on the sides using rooting scissors.

TIP

The trick here is to not let the roots loosen up too much.

3 Appearance after the root cutting is completed.

4 Prepare the pot and add the soil (akadama medium grain 70%, river sand 30%; add around 10% bamboo charcoal and mix well).

TIP

Don't put the bamboo charcoal on the surface of the soil; it will float if you immerse the pot in water.

5 Move the tree and cover the roots with soil (akadama small grain 70%, river sand 30%) and bamboo skewer, making sure to cover so that there are no gaps on the surface.

6 Appearance after the transplanting is completed.

SPROUT PLUCKING (MID APRIL)

1 Use tweezers to grasp sprouts that are too long and break them halfway.

MEMO

Difference in types of leaves

The leaves of Goyoumatsu are considered good when straight (right photo). When choosing a tree, avoid those with curved/curled leaves (left photo). No matter how many years you spend growing the tree, its leaves will not become straight.

Moyogi, 8½ in (21 cm) height, glazed vermilion pot

Shinpaku 真柏

PROFILE

OTHER NAMES Miyama Byakushin
CLASS Cypress (evergreen)
TREE SHAPE Shakan, Chokkan, Soukan, Moyogi, Kengai, Ishitsuki and others

Produce a dark, old tree using Jin and Shari sculptures

From Hokkaido to Takayama in Kyushu, this naturally grows as if rising out of rocky ground. Shinpaku is often called the "true oak," a name that conveys deep respect. Branches are very soft, making it easy to arrange them in many desired shapes. Since it strongly withstands incision and cuts, it's very well suited to Jin and Shari. Also, since the tree itself is very strong, it's very easy to grow even for beginners.

ACTION CALENDAR	Jan		Mar	Apr	May	Jun	Jul	Aug	Sep	Oct	Nov	Dec
			Trans-planting					Transplanting				
					Sprout plucking							
					Fertiliz-ing				Fertilizing			
	Wire placing/ removal											

MANAGEMENT TIPS

Placement Place in a well-ventilated and well-lit place. It can also be raised in partial shade.

Watering Give plenty of water. Water the leaves too during summer.

Fertilizing Use the hard type. Because this tree is such a strong grower, if too much fertilizer is used the roots will become too thick.

Pest Damage Be careful about spider mites. Spritz the leaves with water to protect.

Transplanting It's easy to replant. In the case of young trees, transplant once every two years; when older, once every three years. The best time is either March or August–September.

MAKING A JIN

Before: Late April

→

After: Late April

→

After: Mid-June

PRUNING (LATE APRIL)

1 Cut unnecessary branches to about halfway with branch-cutting scissors.

2 Appearance after pruning is completed.

CREATING JIN/SHARI (LATE APRIL)

1 Peel the bark off the trunk with pincers.

2 Carve the peeled part with branch-cutting scissors again.

TIP

Avoid leaving cut marks and direct scissors to make the carving look natural.

MEMO

Be careful not to peel too much!

Trees absorb moisture and nutrients through the soft part of the skin and support the body of the tree from the inside, like a skeleton. In spring, the trunk drinks in moisture and the bark is very soft, so excessive peeling can damage the trunk; on the other hand, peeling the bark is difficult in winter.

TIP

Do not forget to protect the wounds.

3 Appearance after the carving is completed.

WIRING/BRANCH ARRANGING (LATE APRIL)

1 Wrap one branch at a time and arrange them.

TIP

The trunk is bent, so you can bend the branch to balance.

2 Appearance after wiring and branch arranging are completed.

TRANSPLANTING (LATE APRIL)

※Transplant in March from the second time onward

1 Scoop the soil away vertically with a rake.

2 Cut long roots using rooting scissors.

3 Appearance of the roots after the cutting is completed.

4 Prepare the pot and the lower soil (80% akadama medium grain; 20% river sand. Add around 10% worth of bamboo charcoal as well).

※Use a mixture of 80% akadama medium grain, 20% river sand, and add about 10% bamboo charcoal.

TIP

Don't place the bamboo charcoal on the surface of the soil; it will float if you immerse the pot in water.

5 Place the top layer of soil (80% akadama small grain; 20% river sand) from the top.

※Use a mixture of 80% akadama small grain, 20% river sand.

6 Appearance after transplanting is completed and moss is spread.

SPROUT PLUCKING (MID-JUNE)

1 Appearance when sprouts are overgrown.

2 Pluck the protruding sprouts with tweezers.

3 Appearance after plucking is completed.

Sugi 杉

PROFILE

OTHER NAMES Susugi, Suguki, Japanese red cedar
CLASS Cypress, *Cryptomeria japonica* (evergreen tall)
TREE SHAPE Chokkan, Soukan, Kabutachi, Yoseue and others

Chokkan, 8 in (20 cm) height, flat pot

Tall, straight and elegant, with color-changing leaves

This tree was originally from Aomori but has become widespread to Yakushima. Some trees are 300–400 years old and are venerated as spiritual trees from a long gone past. When planted, these trees grow upright; however, when they grow naturally in a forest, they grow in various elegant shapes. It's charming, the way their leaves subtly change in color depending on the season.

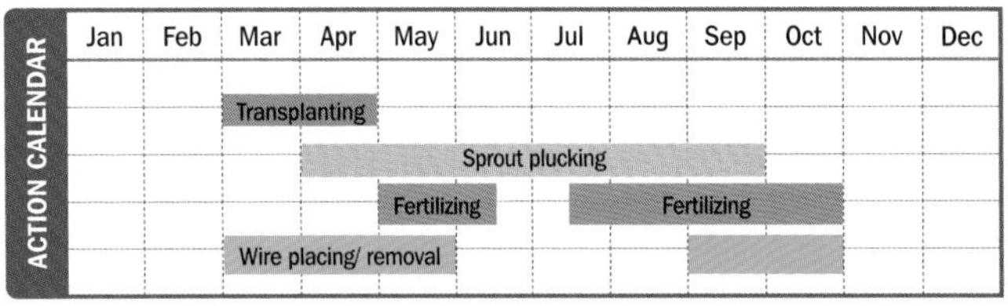

MANAGEMENT TIPS

Placement Place the tree in a well-ventilated place with good sunlight. It can also grow in partial shade.

Watering It likes water. Depending on the season, the number of times you water it in a week changes.

Fertilizing Give solid fertilizer. If given too much, the branches and leaves will overgrow so be moderate.

Pest Damage Be careful of spider mites, soot and red withering diseases. Spritz leaves with water to protect from spider mites.

Transplanting If young, transplant once every two years; if older, once every three years. The ideal time is March to April.

TRANSPLANTING IN A FLAT POT AND PLACING A KUZUYA

Before: Late April

→

After: Late April

PRUNING (LATE APRIL)

1 Prune branches that are too crowded with leaves using pruning scissors. Cut the tip of the pruned branches.

TIP

Since the trunk of this species is thin, take care of the balance of the whole tree and reduce the leaves.

2 Appearance after pruning.

TIP

Try to make it so that the base of the branches on the trunk can be visible.

WIRING/BRANCH ARRANGING (LATE APRIL)

1 Wrap one branch at a time and arrange them.

2 Appearance after wiring is completed.

TRANSPLANTING (LATE APRIL)

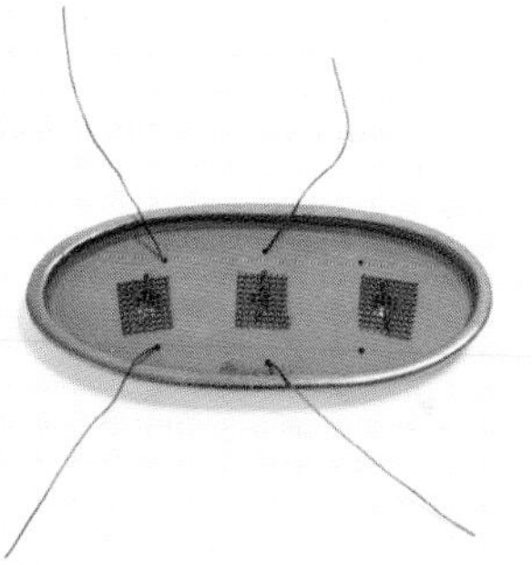

1 Prepare the pot and the lower soil (80% akadama medium grain; 20% river sand. Add around 10% worth of bamboo charcoal as well).

※Use a mixture of 80% akadama medium grain, 20% river sand, and add about 10% bamboo charcoal.

2 Place the tree in advance in the pot, position it, and gauge the amount of soil that might be needed.

3 Remove the tree and place the soil on the bottom.

4 Fix the tree in two points and tighten the wire with pliers.

TIP

Don't place bamboo charcoal on the surface of the soil; it will float if you immerse the pot in water.

5 Place the top layer of soil (80% akadama small grain; 20% river sand) from the top.

TIP

Sprout plucking is the same as for Toshou.

6 Appearance after transplanting is completed, moss is spread and a Kuzuya is added.

MEMO

Creating a narrative by using Kuzuya!

Kuzuya is an old ornament such as the one pictured here. They add charm and texture to sparser landscapes. When considering the bonsai as a scene, little ornaments like this can help create a narrative.

Kabutachi, 8 in (20 cm) height, Shudei round pot

Sekkahinoki 石化檜

PROFILE

OTHER NAMES Kujakuhiba, Ougonhinoki, Nana, Chabohiba.
CLASS Hinoki
TREE SHAPE Chokkan, Soukan, Shakan, Yoseue and others

Dense, scaly leaves suitable for a small bonsai

Hinoki grows in Honshu, Shikoku and Kyushu. It is often used for building. In the bonsai world, Sekkahinoki and Tsuyamahinoki appear very frequently. Sekkahinoki is a tree with dense scale-like leaves and is very suitable as a small bonsai. If sprout plucking is done routinely, it will prevent sprouts from withering and the tree will have a clean, beautiful outline.

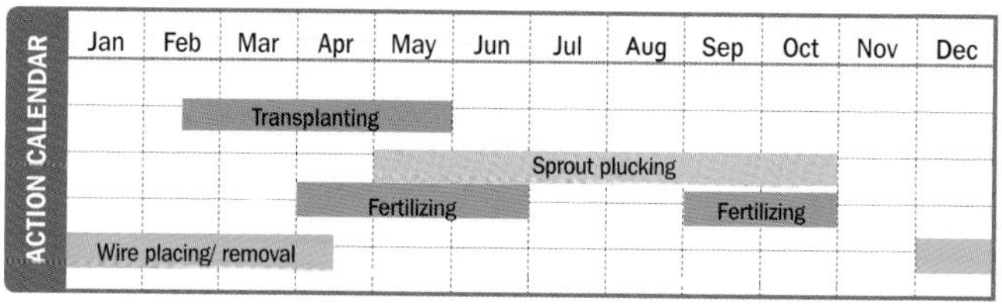

MANAGEMENT TIPS

Placement Place the tree in a well-ventilated place with good sunlight. Move it to partial shade from December to protect the scaly green leaves.

Watering It likes water. Water when the surface of the soil is dry.

Fertilizing It likes fertilizer. Use the solid type.

Pest Damage Be careful of spider mites and ladybugs. Spritz leaves with water to protect from spider mites.

Transplanting If young, transplant once every two years. If older, once every three years. The ideal time is between mid-February and May.

MAKING A SOUKAN

Before: Mid-February

→

After: Mid-February

PRUNING (MID-FEBRUARY)

1 Cut overgrown branches using pruning shears.

TIP

Putting strain on the branches will make the future branches thicker.

2 Appearance after pruning.

WIRING (MID-FEBRUARY)

1 Wrap one branch at a time and arrange them.

TIP

Since the branches are soft, they are easy to arrange. Since the leaves are thin, the shape of the tree is mostly dependent on the branches.

2 Remove leaves that have grown on the lower side of the branches using tweezers.

3 Appearance after the wiring and leaf removal are completed.

TRANSPLANTING (MID-FEBRUARY)

1 Scoop the soil away downwards with a rake and cut long roots using rooting scissors.

2 Appearance of the roots after the cutting is completed.

3 Prepare the pot and the lower soil (80% akadama medium grain; 20% river sand. Add around 10% worth of bamboo charcoal as well).

※Use a mixture of 80% akadama medium grain, 20% river sand, and add about 10% bamboo charcoal.

TIP

Don't place the bamboo charcoal on the surface of the soil; it will float if you immerse the pot in water.

4 Bend the wire with pliers to fix the tree and cut the excess wire. Then add the top layer of soil (80% akadama small grain; 20% river sand) from the top.

※Use a mixture of 80% akadama small grain, 20% river sand.

5 Appearance after transplanting is completed and moss is spread.

MEMO

Pluck the sprouts and align the outline

In mid-June the sprouts start to overgrow. Pluck out the ones that stick out or create imbalance.

(Before and after plucking)

Hankengai, 11 in (28 cm) height, Chinese pot

Tsuyama Hinok 津山檜

PROFILE

OTHER NAMES Chabohiba
CLASS Hinoki
TREE SHAPE Chokkan, Soukan, Shakan, Yoseue and others

Discovered and grown in Okayama, this bonsai is charming, with its fine, dense leaves

This bonsai was discovered in the Tsuyama district in the Okayama Prefecture and has been bred ever since. Compared to Sekka-hinoki it has finer and denser leaves. This bonsai's popularity has become widespread throughout Japan.

<table>
<tr><th>ACTION CALENDAR</th><th>Jan</th><th>Feb</th><th>Mar</th><th>Apr</th><th>May</th><th>Jun</th><th>Jul</th><th>Aug</th><th>Sep</th><th>Oct</th><th>Nov</th><th>Dec</th></tr>
<tr><td></td><td></td><td colspan="4">Transplanting</td><td></td><td></td><td></td><td></td><td></td><td></td><td></td></tr>
<tr><td></td><td></td><td></td><td></td><td></td><td colspan="6">Sprout plucking</td><td></td><td></td></tr>
<tr><td></td><td></td><td></td><td></td><td colspan="3">Fertilizing</td><td></td><td></td><td colspan="2">Fertilizing</td><td></td><td></td></tr>
<tr><td></td><td colspan="4">Wire placing/ removal</td><td></td><td></td><td></td><td></td><td></td><td></td><td></td><td></td></tr>
</table>

MANAGEMENT TIPS

Placement Place the tree in a well-ventilated place with good sunlight. Move it to partial shade from December to protect the scaly green leaves.

Watering It likes water. Water generously when the surface of the soil is dry.

Fertilizing It likes fertilizer. Use the solid type.

Pest Damage Be careful of spider mites and ladybugs. Spritz leaves with water to protect from spider mites.

Transplanting If young, transplant once every two years; if older, once every three years. The ideal time is between mid-February and May.

MAKING A CHOKKAN

Before: Mid-April

→

After: Mid-April

PRELIMINARY WORK (MID-APRIL)

1 Prepare a large pot and put newspaper between the pot and the roots to fix the tree in an upright position.

TIP

This tree was planted on a diagonal. This step will realign the tree so that it is straight.

PRUNING (MID-APRIL)

1 Prune branches that have gotten too heavy with branch-cutting scissors.

2 Appearance after pruning.

WIRING (MID-APRIL)

1 Wrap one branch at a time and arrange the branches.

2 Appearance after the wiring and arranging are completed.

TRANSPLANTING (MID-APRIL)

1 Remove the tree from the pot.

TIP

You can see that the roots were taking the shape of the pot.

2 Cut the roots vertically using rooting scissors.

3 Appearance after pruning.

4 Appearance after the roots have been scooped.

5 Prepare the pot and the lower soil (80% akadama medium grain; 20% river sand. Add around 10% worth of bamboo charcoal as well).

※Use a mixture of 80% akadama medium grain, 20% river sand, and add about 10% bamboo charcoal.

TIP

Don't place the bamboo charcoal on the surface of the soil; it will float if you immerse the pot in water.

6 Put the rest of the soil* on the top and make sure there are no gaps, using tweezers or a bamboo skewer.

※Use a mixture of 80% akadama small grain, 20% river sand.

7 Appearance after transplanting is completed and moss is spread.

TIP

Sprout plucking (mid-June) is done in the same way as for Sekkahinoki (p. 85).

Moyogi, 3½ in (9 cm) height, Chinese pot

Toshou 杜松

PROFILE

OTHER NAMES Nezumisashi, Nezu, Muro, Moroniko
CLASS Hinoki
TREE SHAPE Chokkan, Soukan, Shakan, Yoseue and others

A fat silhouette with needle-like leaves

It grows on the mountains, hills and coasts of Japan. Pointy leaves are gathered in a needle-like fashion, giving the tree a sharp look. It often dominates decor, owing to its strong presence. The branches wither easily, making it especially easy to decorate this tree with Jin and Shari. Trees with leaves as fine as shown in the photo are small and easy to care for.

ACTION CALENDAR

Jan	Feb	Mar	Apr	May	Jun	Jul	Aug	Sep	Oct	Nov	Dec
		Transplanting									
			Sprout plucking								
			Fertilizing					Fertilizing			
Wire placing/ removal											

MANAGEMENT TIPS

Placement Under sunlight and in a well-ventilated spot. It's strong against heat but weak against cold.

Watering Whenever the surface of the soil is dry, give plenty of water.

Fertilizing Use solid fertilizer once a month between April and fall.

Pest Damage Be careful of spider mites, red spider mites and ladybugs. Spritz leaves with water to protect from mites. Spray insecticide if they appear..

Transplanting If young, transplant once every two years; if older, once every three years. The ideal time is between March and April.

MAKING A FUKINAGASHI (BLOWN BY WIND)

Before: Mid-November

→

After: Mid-November

→

After: Early June

PRUNING (MID-NOVEMBER)

1 Remove withered and old (from the previous year) leaves with tweezers.

2 Cut unnecessary branches pointing downward using pruning shears.

TIP

Prune in order to get a Fukinagashi.

3 Appearance after pruning is completed.

WIRING (MID-NOVEMBER)

1 Wrap one branch at a time and arrange the branches.

2 Appearance after the wiring and arranging are completed.

CLEANING A JIN (MID-NOVEMBER)

1 Clean a Jin using high-pressure water.

2 Appearance five months after the Jin has been cleaned.

SPROUT PLUCKING (LATE APRIL)

TIP

Repeat this process at least 4–5 times until September.

1 Gently press on the base of new sprouts with tweezers and pull them out with your fingertips.

SPROUT CUTTING (MID-JUNE)

1 Wrap one branch at a time and arrange the branches.

TIP

During this step, be careful to not accidentally cut any leaves.

2 Using pruning scissors, cut the shaft of the longer sprouts.

3 Appearance after cutting the sprouts.

MEMO

Differences in leaf type

Despite both being Toshou, there are those with thin/fine leaves (photo on the left) and those with coarse leaves (on the right). The Toshou with fine leaves are better suited to become small bonsai, while those with rough leaves are more suited to have Jin and Shari due to their wild appearance.

Isozanshou 磯山椒

Blooming is in mid-May

Hankengai, 8 in (20 cm) height,
12 in (30 cm) width, glazed pot

PROFILE

OTHER NAMES Ten no Ume, Ten no Ubai
CLASS Rosaceae (small evergreen)
TREE SHAPE Hankengai, Shakan, Moyogi and others

Ashy leaves and charming white flowers that inspire love

This grows on the seaside and coral reefs of Okinawa, Kagoshima and Amami. It is so named because its leaves resemble Japanese Prickly Ash (Sanshou 山椒). Despite growing in warm climates, it's strong against cold and can survive inside greenhouses even in cold winters. When leaf cutting is done in February and March, springtime blooming becomes uniform—small white flowers and crimson fruits.

ACTIVITY CALENDAR

<table>
<tr><th>Jan</th><th>Feb</th><th>Mar</th><th>Apr</th><th>May</th><th>Jun</th><th>Jul</th><th>Aug</th><th>Sep</th><th>Oct</th><th>Nov</th><th>Dec</th></tr>
<tr><td></td><td colspan="2">Leaf cutting</td><td colspan="5">Transplanting</td><td>Leaf cutting</td><td></td><td></td><td></td></tr>
<tr><td></td><td></td><td></td><td colspan="5">Sprout plucking</td><td></td><td></td><td></td><td></td></tr>
<tr><td></td><td></td><td></td><td colspan="6">Fertilizing</td><td></td><td></td><td></td></tr>
<tr><td></td><td></td><td colspan="5">Wire placing/ removal</td><td></td><td></td><td></td><td></td><td></td></tr>
</table>

MANAGEMENT TIPS

Placement Place in a well-ventilated and well-lit place. During summer, avoid late afternoon sunlight. Move it to a greenhouse before the first frost.

Watering It likes water. Especially in summer, water 2–3 times per day.

Fertilizing Use solid fertilizer.

Pest Damage It's mostly safe from pest damage.

Transplanting Once every two years. The ideal time is between March and August.

MAKING A MOYOGI

Before: Late March

→

After: Late March

→

After: Mid-June

LEAF CUTTING (LATE MARCH)

1 Cut leaves at their base with leaf-cutting scissors.

TIP

Since the leaves on top are stronger, spread the sprouts uniformly.

2 Appearance after leaf cutting. Unneces-sary standing branch-es can be seen.

PRUNING (LATE MARCH)

1 Cut unnecessary standing branches using pruning shears.

TIP

Apply a healing agent on the wounds.

2 Appearance after pruning.

WIRING (LATE MARCH)

1 Wrap one branch at a time and arrange the branches.

2 Appearance after the wiring and arranging are completed.

TRANSPLANTING (LATE MARCH)

1 Cut long roots using rooting scissors.

2 Cut the main root using pruning scissors.

3 Appearance after the root has been cut.

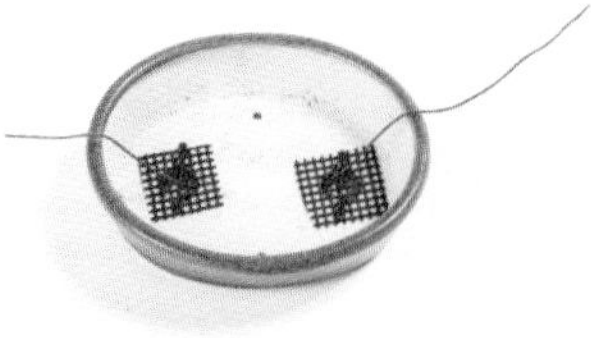

4 Prepare the pot and add the soil (akadama medium grain 80%, river sand 20%; add around 10% bamboo charcoal and mix together).

※Use a mixture of 80% akadama medium grain, 20% river sand, and add about 10% bamboo charcoal.

5 Place the tree and cover with some soil.

TIP

Don't place the bamboo charcoal on the surface of the soil; it will float if you immerse the pot in water.

6 Put the rest of the soil* on the top and make sure there are no gaps, using tweezers or a bamboo skewer.

※Use a mixture of 80% akadama small grain, 20% river sand.

7 Appearance after the transplanting is completed, with moss spread on the soil.

SPROUT CUTTING (MID-MAY)

1 Cut the overgrown sprouts using pruning scissors.

WIRING/BRANCH ARRANGING (MID-JUNE)

1 Wrap new branches (from this year) one by one and arrange them.

2 Appearance after wiring and arranging are completed.

Kabutachi, 9 in (23 cm) height, pale pot

Ichou 銀杏

PROFILE

OTHER NAMES Ginkgo biloba
CLASS Ginkgo
TREE SHAPE Chokkan, Shakan, Yoseue and others

Enjoy the colors of every season

Originally from China, it's said that one in every ten trees in Japan's side streets is an Ichou. Starting in a small, cute shape in late April, it gradually gets larger until it reaches its normal size. Afterward, its appearance changes each season and cycles from green leaves to yellow leaves to a bare tree, truly remaining charming throughout the year. And being very robust, it's very easy for beginners to grow.

ACTION CALENDAR

<table>
<tr><th>Jan</th><th>Feb</th><th>Mar</th><th>Apr</th><th>May</th><th>Jun</th><th>Jul</th><th>Aug</th><th>Sep</th><th>Oct</th><th>Nov</th><th>Dec</th></tr>
<tr><td></td><td></td><td colspan="2">Transplanting</td><td></td><td></td><td></td><td></td><td></td><td></td><td></td><td></td></tr>
<tr><td></td><td></td><td></td><td colspan="2">Sprout plucking</td><td></td><td></td><td></td><td></td><td></td><td></td><td></td></tr>
<tr><td></td><td></td><td></td><td colspan="3">Fertilizing</td><td></td><td></td><td colspan="2">Fertilizing</td><td></td><td></td></tr>
<tr><td></td><td colspan="2">Wire placing/ removal</td><td></td><td></td><td></td><td></td><td></td><td></td><td></td><td></td><td></td></tr>
</table>

MANAGEMENT TIPS

Placement Place in a well-ventilated and well-lit place. During summer, avoid late afternoon sunlight. During winter, move it under cover.

Watering Be careful to not forget to water it during the summer. Sprinkle the leaves in evenings.

Fertilizing Use solid fertilizer.

Pest Damage Be careful of bagworm moths and sooty mold.

Transplanting If it's young, do this once every two years; if old, once every three years. The best time is between March and April.

TRANSPLANTING IN AN ELLIPTICAL POT

Before: Late March

→

After: Late March

→

After: Mid-May

PRUNING (LATE MARCH)

1 If there's an old cut wound in the main trunk, cut it obliquely with branch-cutting scissors.

2 Cut unnecessary overlapping branches with branching scissors.

3 Using a brush, apply a healing agent on the wounds.

WIRING/BRANCH ARRANGING (LATE MARCH)

1 Wrap one branch at a time and arrange them.

TIP

Since the branches are very narrow, try to spread the branches during this step.

2 Appearance after wiring is completed.

TRANSPLANTING (LATE MARCH)

TIP

Thick roots may grow and break the pot to keep growing so definitely cut them.

1 Scoop the soil away downwards with a rake. Cut the long roots and if there's any thick roots, cut those too.

2 Appearance after cutting the thick root.

3 Appearance after cutting all the unnecessary roots.

4 Prepare the pot and add the soil (akadama medium grain 80%, river sand 20%; add around 10% bamboo charcoal and mix together).

※Use a mixture of 80% akadama medium grain, 20% river sand, and add about 10% bamboo charcoal.

5 Appearance after the transplanting is completed, with moss spread on the soil.

MEMO

Distinguishing male and female trees

As shown in the photo below, you can get a sense of the tree's gender by observing the shape of the leaves, although the pollen cone in males and ovules in females are a more obvious clue.

Male trees = Leaves tend to be deeply notched.

Female trees = Leaves tend to be more regularly fan-shaped.

Soukan, 6¾ in (17 cm) height, Tofukuji elliptical pot

Ibota 水蠟

PROFILE

OTHER NAMES Kogomebana, Konezu, Ibotanoki
CLASS Moxaceaceae
TREE SHAPE Shakan, Kabutachi, Moyogi, Kengai and others

Robust, easy to raise and fun to care for

A strong grower throughout Japan. If you choose a rugged variety, the trunk ages faster and it takes on a mellow tone. The thin, delicate branches have a particular charm, and if leaves are cut frequently, they will become denser. The tiny white flowers and fruits are especially stylish as they take on a purplish hue.

ACTIVITY CALENDAR

Jan	Feb	Mar	Apr	May	Jun	Jul	Aug	Sep	Oct	Nov	Dec
	Transplanting				Transplanting Leaf cutting						
			Sprout plucking								
			Fertilizing						Fertilizing		
					Wire placing/ removal				Wire placing/ removal		

MANAGEMENT TIPS

Placement If you want a thick trunk, place in a sunny place; if instead you want to increase the branches, place in the shade.

Watering It's resistant to drought. The amount of water required depends on the growth of the tree.

Fertilizing Give solid fertilizer.

Pest Damage Be careful of beetles.

Transplanting Once per year. Either between February and mid-April or between June and July.

PREPARING A KABUTACHI

Before: Early June

→

After: Early June

PRUNING (EARLY JUNE)

1 Cut the overgrown branches using pruning shears.

LEAF CUTTING (EARLY JUNE)

1 Cut the bigger leaves with leaf-cutting scissors.

TRANSPLANTING (EARLY JUNE)

1 Scoop the soil away downwards with a rake.

2 Cut the long roots using pruning scissors.

TIP

Since the roots are very thick, pruning scissors will work just as well as rooting scissors.

3 Appearance after the roots have been cut.

4 Prepare the pot and add the soil (akadama medium grain 80%, river sand 20%; add around 10% bamboo charcoal and mix together).

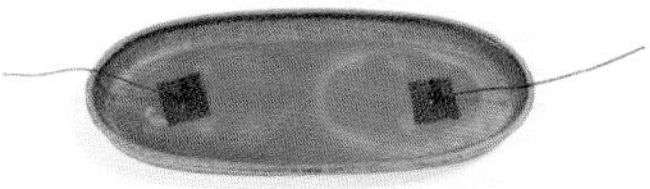

※Use a mixture of 80% akadama medium grain, 20% river sand, and add about 10% bamboo charcoal.

5 Place the tree and the rest of the soil.

6 Appearance after transplanting is completed.

Yoseue, 7½ in (19 cm) height

Iwashide 岩四手

PROFILE

OTHER NAMES Soro, Koshide
CLASS Birchaceae
TREE SHAPE Kabutachi, Yoseue and others

Create a wonderful atmosphere with Kabutachi or Yoseue shapes

If shaped as Kabutachi or Yoseue, this tree will become one truly amazing bonsai. If it's a Yoseue, even 4–5-year-old stumps are spectacular to see, but they can also be appreciated when young. You can enjoy observing the cycle of seasons on your own tree, going from budding in spring to beautiful red leaves in the fall. When the tree becomes very old, a striped pattern appears on the trunk, making it even more lovely.

<table>
<tr><th>ACTIVITY CALENDAR</th><th>Jan</th><th>Feb</th><th>Mar</th><th>Apr</th><th>May</th><th>Jun</th><th>Jul</th><th>Aug</th><th>Sep</th><th>Oct</th><th>Nov</th><th>Dec</th></tr>
<tr><td></td><td></td><td colspan="3">Transplanting</td><td>Leaf cutting</td><td></td><td></td><td></td><td></td><td></td><td></td><td></td></tr>
<tr><td></td><td></td><td></td><td></td><td colspan="3">Sprout plucking</td><td></td><td></td><td></td><td></td><td></td><td></td></tr>
<tr><td></td><td></td><td></td><td></td><td colspan="3">Fertilizing</td><td></td><td></td><td colspan="2">Fertilizing</td><td></td><td></td></tr>
<tr><td></td><td colspan="3">Wire placing/ removal</td><td></td><td></td><td></td><td></td><td></td><td></td><td></td><td></td><td></td></tr>
</table>

MANAGEMENT TIPS

Placement Place in a well-ventilated and well-lit place. Avoid direct sunlight in the summer and move the plant inside or under cover during winter.

Watering Water frequently, be careful of drainage during summer. It can cause leaf burns.

Fertilizing Use solid fertilizer.

Pest Damage Be careful of aphids, bear beetles, scale insects and powdery mildew.

Transplanting If it's young, do this once every two years; if old, once every three years. The best time is between February and April.

MAKING A KABUTACHI

Before: Late March

→

After: Late March

→

After: Mid-June

PRUNING (LATE MARCH)

1 Cut the branches disturbing the flow of the tree shape using pruning scissors.

> **TIP**
>
> *In addition, for sprouts that are directly at the base of branches, cut the branch and clear up the space around the branch.*

2 Appearance after pruning is completed.

WIRING/BRANCH ARRANGING (LATE MARCH)

1 Wrap one branch at a time and arrange them.

2 Appearance after wiring is completed.

TRANSPLANTING (LATE MARCH)

1 Shorten the roots using rooting scissors.

2 Appearance after shortening the roots.

3 Prepare the pot and add the soil (akadama medium grain 80%, river sand 20%; add around 10% bamboo charcoal and mix together).

※Use a mixture of 80% akadama medium grain, 20% river sand, and add about 10% bamboo charcoal.

4 Appearance after the transplanting is completed, with moss spread on the soil.

SPROUT CUTTING (MID-MAY)

1 Appearance of grown sprouts.

2 Cut overgrown sprouts using pruning scissors.

SPROUT CUTTING (MID-JUNE)

1 Cut overgrown sprouts using pruning scissors.

2 Appearance after cutting the sprouts.

Moyoki, 6 in (15 cm) height, Chinese pot

Egonoki えごのき

PROFILE

OTHER NAMES Rokurogi, Chishanoki
CLASS Styracaceae
TREE SHAPE Moyogi, Shakan, Kengai, BunJingi and others

Elegant and charming, with sweet, hanging flowers

This grows everywhere in Japan from Hokkaido to Okinawa. It's commonly called "Snowbell" because of its lovely white or pinkish clusters of hanging blossoms. Along with the flowers, which bloom in early summer, a little oval fruit also grows.

<table>
<tr><th>ACTION CALENDAR</th><th>Jan</th><th>Feb</th><th>Mar</th><th>Apr</th><th>May</th><th>Jun</th><th>Jul</th><th>Aug</th><th>Sep</th><th>Oct</th><th>Nov</th><th>Dec</th></tr>
<tr><td></td><td></td><td colspan="3">Transplanting</td><td></td><td></td><td></td><td></td><td></td><td></td><td></td><td></td></tr>
<tr><td></td><td></td><td></td><td></td><td colspan="4">Sprout plucking</td><td></td><td></td><td></td><td></td><td></td></tr>
<tr><td></td><td></td><td></td><td></td><td></td><td colspan="3">Fertilizing</td><td></td><td colspan="2">Fertilizing</td><td></td><td></td></tr>
<tr><td></td><td colspan="7">Wire placing/ removal</td><td></td><td></td><td></td><td></td><td></td></tr>
</table>

MANAGEMENT TIPS

Placement Place in a well-ventilated and well-lit place. During summer avoid late afternoon sunlight.

Watering Be careful not to neglect watering this tree. If it dries, the leaves end up bending backwards.

Fertilizing Use solid fertilizer.

Pest Damage Be careful of bagworm moths and sooty mold.

Transplanting Once every two years. The best time is between February and April.

PREPARING A HANKENGAI

Before: Early April

→

After: Early April

→

After: Mid-May

WIRING/BRANCH ARRANGING (EARLY APRIL)

1 Wrap one branch at a time and arrange them.

2 Appearance after wiring and branch arrangement are completed.

TRANSPLANTING (EARLY APRIL)

1 Cut the upper part of the roots using rooting scissors.

2 Cut the roots on the sides using rooting scissors.

3 Appearance after the root cutting is completed.

4 Prepare the pot and add the soil (akadama medium grain 80%, river sand 20%).

※Use a mixture of 80% akadama medium grain, 20% river sand.

5 Appearance after transplanting is completed and moss is spread.

SPROUT PLUCKING (MID-MAY)

1 Appearance when sprouts are overgrown.

2 Pluck the protruding sprouts with tweezers.

TIP

By removing a growth point, you can stop a sprout's growth.

WIRING/BRANCH ARRANGING (MID MAY)

1 Wrap one branch at a time and arrange them.

2 Appearance after wiring and branch arrangement are completed.

Kuchinashi 梔子

Moyogi, 6¾ in (17 cm) height.

PROFILE

OTHER NAMES *Gardenia jasminoides*
CLASS Rubia
TREE SHAPE Kabutachi, Moyogi and others

Choose the variety of leaves you prefer

This grows glossy leaves, pure white flowers and orange fruits. In a single blossoming you'll find slender, round and squared leaves. The beauty and fragrance of the flowers compensates for the lack of a second blossoming. If replanted after cutting the leaves, the sprouts' quality will increase. It is robust, easy to raise, and fast-growing.

ACTIVITY CALENDAR

Jan	Feb	Mar	Apr	May	Jun	Jul	Aug	Sep	Oct	Nov	Dec
			Transplanting								
				Leaf cutting							
					Sprout plucking						
					Fertilizing			Fertilizing			
			Wire placing/ removal								

MANAGEMENT TIPS

Placement Place in a well-ventilated and well-lit place. Shield it from direct sunlight in the summer to avoid leaf burn. Move inside or to under the cover during winter.

Watering Be careful to not let it dry out during summer.

Fertilizing If given too much fertilizer the fruits will be ruined. You can also opt not to use any fertilizer at all.

Pest Damage Be careful of caterpillar larvae.

Transplanting Once every two years. The best time is between April and May.

MAKING A HANKENGAI

Before: Early April

→

After: Early April

LEAF CUTTING (EARLY APRIL)

TIP

The reason we cut the leaves in the first place is that not doing makes branch pruning difficult.

1 Cut the leaves with leaf-cutting scissors and prune the unnecessary branches using pruning shears.

WIRING/BRANCH ARRANGING (EARLY APRIL)

1 Wrap one branch at a time and arrange thcm.

2 Appearance after wiring and branch arrangement are completed.

TRANSPLANTING (EARLY APRIL)

TIP

Cutting the curved roots makes it easier to scoop them later.

1 Cut the roots vertically using rooting scissors.

2 Scoop the soil away vertically with a rake then cut long roots using rooting scissors.

3 Appearance after the root cutting is completed.

※Use a mixture of 80% akadama medium grain, 20% river sand, and add about 10% bamboo charcoal.

4 Prepare the pot and the lower soil (80% akadama medium grain; 20% river sand. Add around 10% worth of bamboo charcoal as well).

5 Appearance after transplanting is completed and moss is spread.

Keyaki 欅

PROFILE

OTHER NAMES Tsuki
CLASS Ulmaceae
TREE SHAPE Hokidachi, Kabutachi, Yoseue and others

Chokkan, 8½ in (22 cm) height, Mossbank pot

Delicate small branches reach up and outward in this popular tree

This tree grows all over the Japanese Mainland. It has an upright trunk and a crown expanding toward the sky that gives off the same vibes that a large tree would. Each season is packed with beautiful sights: young leaves, yellow leaves or maybe a bare tree. Repeating blossoming and leaf cutting very often are the trick to truly exposing the beauty of this tree.

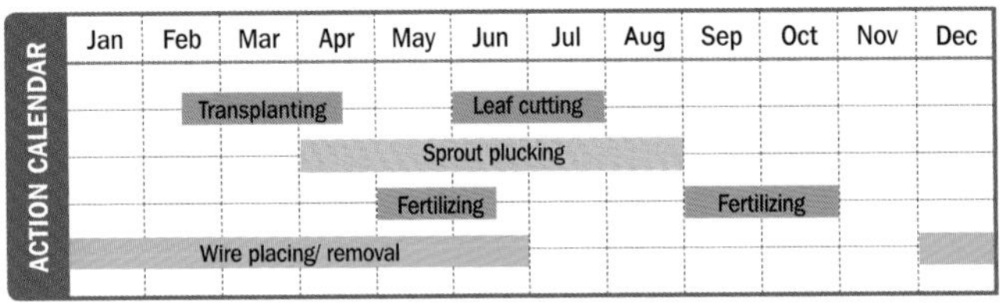

MANAGEMENT TIPS

Placement Place in a well-ventilated and well-lit place. If left in the shade, the branches won't grow dense.

Watering Give plenty of water daily.

Fertilizing Give solid fertilizer. Too much fertlizer will cause the branches to grow too much.

Pest Damage Be careful of aphids. Use fungicidal insecticide.

Transplanting If young, transplant once every two years; if old, once every three years. The ideal time is March to April.

REARRANGING IN A HEIBACHI

Before: Late April

Before: Early June

After: Mid-June

SPROUT PLUCKING (MID-MAY)

1 Remove overgrown sprouts with tweezers.

MEMO

Trim/pluck frequently when the sprouts grow

Doing this will make the branches thicker and more robust. Each sprout will bud more than once, so wait for them to regrow and remove them each time (usually two or three times).

Budding usually starts from the stronger parts and spreads through the rest of the tree, influencing the amount of foliage growth. The foundation of working on bonsai is making sure it's uniform and balanced.

SPROUT CUTTING (EARLY JUNE)

1 Cut unnecessary sprouts using pruning scissors.

2 Appearance after cutting is completed.

LEAF CUTTING (EARLY JUNE)

1 Cut leaves at their base with leaf-cutting scissors.

2 Appearance after leaf cutting is completed.

PRUNING (EARLY JUNE)

1 Cut thick branches using pruning scissors.

2 Cut branches pointing downward using pruning scissors.

3 Cut unnecessary branches using pruning scissors.

4 Appearance after pruning.

TIP

In the case of the Keyaki, all branches divide into two. The trunk also divides into two. An ideal situation is when one sub-branch and sub-trunk is thicker than the other.

MEMO

When pruning, don't trim the whole outline of the tree.

In the state after pruning, occasionally leave some hanging branches despite their effect on the balance of the tree (as shown here). The reason for this is that we will wire them later on.

WIRING/BRANCH ARRANGING (EARLY APRIL)

1 Wrap one branch at a time and arrange them.

TIP

Wiring while you lower the branches will allow your fingers to pass through easily. When arranging the branches, raise the branches back up.

2 Appearance after wiring and branch arranging are completed.

MEMO

Wiring is best done in early summer

The perfect time for wiring is at the beginning of summer. If done right after leaf cutting, the branches are wet, soft and flexible, making it very easy to wrap wire and arrange them.

During winter, since the branches are dry, wiring should be avoided. (Timing is key to all of the processes in bonsai!)

TRANSPLANTING (EARLY JUNE)

※Usually it's done between February and April, but it's also okay to transplant after leaf cutting.

1 Clean the roots with a wire brush.

TIP

If the surface of the soil is made smooth, the roots will emerge.

2 Appearance after the roots emerged.

3 Cut the corners of the surface using pruning scissors.

TIP

Since the roots are thin, rooting scissors aren't necessary.

4 Cut the sides of the roots using pruning scissors.

5 Scoop the roots downwards with a rake.

6 Appearance after step **5**.

7 Prepare the pot and the soil.

※Use akadama medium grain 80%; river sand 20%. Add around 10% worth of bamboo charcoal into the mix as well.

8 Place the soil in the center of the pot and gather it in a hill shape.

TIP

As the tree is planted, it will push the soil to the sides.

9 Align with the soil on the bottom of the pot, cut the bottom of the roots using pruning scissors and make a hollow space.

10 Place the top layer of soil (80% akadama small grain; 20% river sand) from the top.

TIP

Don't place the bamboo charcoal on the surface of the soil; it will float if you immerse the pot in water.

11 Use tweezers to make sure there are no gaps in the soil that and it's evenly spread.

12 Appearance after transplanting is completed and moss is spread.

SPROUT PLUCKING (MID-MAY)

1 State of the branches grown out.

2 Pluck the overgrown branches with tweezers.

3 Appearancc after sprout plucking.

Konara 小楢

PROFILE

OTHER NAMES Hooso (Hahaso), Nara
CLASS Beech Family (Fagaceae)
TREE SHAPE Moyogi, Kabutachi, Kengai, Yoseue and others

Flowers blooming in late April

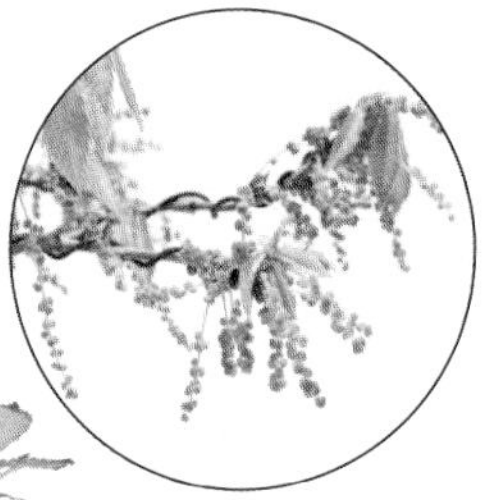

Fruits starting to appear in mid-June

Hankengai, 7 in (18 cm) height, 13 in (33 cm) width, Japanese pot

Overflowing with rustic and nostalgic beauty

This tree grows all over Japan. It's strong and easy to grow. It is similar to the Donguri (Acorn), but it's not very common as a bonsai. The changes that come with each season are particularly beautiful.

ACTION CALENDAR

Jan	Feb	Mar	Apr	May	Jun	Jul	Aug	Sep	Oct	Nov	Dec
		Transplanting	Transplanting								
			Sprout plucking	Sprout plucking							
					Fertilizing			Fertilizing	Fertilizing		
Wire placing/ removal	Wire placing/ removal	Wire placing/ removal	Wire placing/ removal	Wire placing/ removal	Wire placing/ removal						Wire placing/ removal

MANAGEMENT TIPS

Placement Place in a well-ventilated and well-lit place. Avoid direct sunlight in the summer and move the plant inside or under cover during winter.

Watering When the surface gets dry, give plenty of water.

Fertilizing Use solid fertilizer.

Pest Damage Be careful of sooty mold.

Transplanting Transplant once a year. The best time is between March and April. Cut thick main roots and leave the thin roots instead.

PREPARING THE TREE SHAPE

Before: Early November

→

Before: Early April

→

After: Early April

PRUNING (EARLY APRIL)

1 Cut the branches that were left uncut at their base with branch-cutting scissors.

WIRING/BRANCH ARRANGING (EARLY APRIL)

1 Wrap one branch at a time and arrange them.

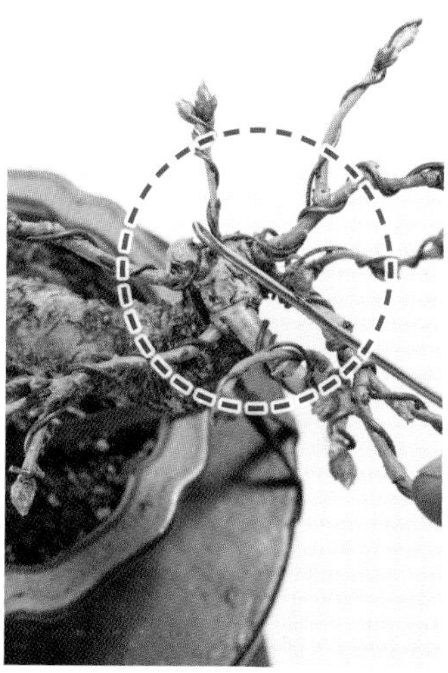

2 After cutting the branches, apply a healing coating agent with a hard brush.

3 Appearance after wiring and arranging are completed.

TRANSPLANTING (EARLY JUNE)

1 Sometimes a main root overgrows.

2 In that case, cut the main root with branch-cutting scissors at its base.

3 Also cut the roots that stick out with branch-cutting scissors.

4 Appearance after scooping the roots downwards with a rake and cutting the longer roots using rooting scissors.

5 Prepare the pot and the soil.

※Use akadama medium grain 80%; river sand 20%.

6 Place the top layer of soil and use tweezers to make sure that there are no gaps in the soil.

※80% akadama small grain; 20% river sand.

7 Appearance after transplanting is completed and moss is spread.

REMOVING THE WIRING (MID-JUNE)

1 Remove the wire that you put on in spring (early April).

TIP

Since Konara grows very quickly, the wire will easily bite into the branches.

Moyogi, 7½ in (19 cm) height,
Kusamoto pot (grass bottom)

Sarusuberi 百日紅

PROFILE

OTHER NAMES Hyakujikkou
CLASS Lythraceae
TREE SHAPE Shakan, BunJingi, Moyogi, Fukinagashi, Kengai and others

Its charm resides in small and delicate branches spreading widely in a smooth trunk

This bonsai is originally from China. It's said that its bright trunk is so smooth that "even monkeys slip on it." Its crimson flowers bloom for a hundred days. The fine branches and unique bark are the main attractions. By giving plenty of fertilizer and cutting sprouts often, the branches will spread and diverge. It is strong and easy to grow.

MANAGEMENT TIPS

Placement Place in a well-ventilated and well-lit place. Move the plant inside or under cover during winter.

Watering It likes water. During the flower budding season (May and June), let it dry a little bit.

Fertilizing Use solid fertilizer.

Pest Damage Be careful of aphids and sooty mold.

Transplanting This is done once a year. The best time is between March and April.

ACTION CALENDAR

Jan	Feb	Mar	Apr	May	Jun	Jul	Aug	Sep	Oct	Nov	Dec
		Transplanting			Leaf cutting						
			Sprout plucking								
				Fertilizing							
			Wire placing/ removal								

MAKING A KABUTACHI

Before: Mid-April

→

After: Mid-April

→

After: Mid-June

WIRING/BRANCH ARRANGING (EARLY APRIL)

1 Wrap one branch at a time and arrange them.

2 Appearance after wiring and branch arranging are completed.

TRANSPLANTING (MID APRIL)

1 Scoop the roots downwards with a rake.

※Since Sashiki has been performed on this tree for the past two years, its roots are thin.

2 Cut the longer roots using rooting scissors.

3 Take the root on top and wrap it very tightly with metal wire to fix it.

4 Entangle the wire in a downward spiral and collect the roots in it.

5 Appearance of the roots pulled together by wire.

6 Prepare the pot and the soil.

※Akadama medium grain 80%; river sand 20%.

7 Tie the roots to thc wire and fix the tree in place.

8 Appearance after transplanting is completed and moss is spread.

PRUNING (EARLY JUNE)

1 Appearance of the tree after the branches grow.

2 Cut any withered branches using pruning scissors.

SPROUT CUTTING (EARLY JUNE)

TIP
Leave two uncut leaves per branch.

1 Using pruning scissors, cut any overgrown sprouts.

2 Appearance after the sprout cutting is completed.

SPROUT CUTTING (MID-JUNE)

1 Appearance of the tree with overgrown sprouts.

2 Using pruning scissors, cut any overgrown sprouts.

TIP
Leave two leaves uncut per branch.

WIRING/BRANCH ARRANGING (EARLY APRIL)

1 Wrap one branch at a time and arrange them.

2 Appearance after wiring and branch arrangement are completed.

TIP
The flowers bloom at the end of August.

Chirimenkazura 縮緬蔓

Shakan, 3½ in (9 cm) height, Keishin pot

PROFILE

OTHER NAMES Choujikazura, Masakikazura
CLASS Dogbanes (Vine-like, Deciduous)
TREE SHAPE Moyogi, Kengai, Soukan, Kabutachi, Ishitsuki

Vine-like robust tree and beautiful glossy small leaves

With small leaves that can be compared to silk, this tree species is very robust and comparable to vines. Being a half-deciduous tree, even during the Momiji season, a part of the leaves remains green. The mixed appearance of these crimson-and-green leaves gives this bonsai a unique charm. If transplanted in a small pot, its leaves will also become smaller, giving them a more delicate look. It's the second fastest tree to enter Momiji (red leaves) season, the fastest one being Hazenoki.

MANAGEMENT TIPS

Placement While growing, place in a well-lit place. After transplanting in a smaller pot, place in half-shade.

Watering It requires plenty of water. In summer, it should be watered both morning and evening. Be more moderate in winter.

Fertilizing It likes fertilizer. While growing, give fertilizer once a month.

Pest Damage Be careful of aphids. Also, be aware that this tree heals from wounds very slowly.

Transplanting Transplant once every two years. The best time is between April and May. Rather than making the roots denser, work instead on making the branches denser and longer.

ACTION CALENDAR

ACTION CALENDAR	Jan	Feb	Mar	Apr	May	Jun	Jul	Aug	Sep	Oct	Nov	Dec
Transplanting				✓	✓							
Sprout plucking				✓	✓	✓	✓					
Fertilizing			✓	✓	✓	✓	✓		✓	✓	✓	
Wire placing/ removal			✓	✓	✓	✓	✓					

TRANSPLANTING AFTER BUDDING

Before: Mid-May

After: Mid-May

TRANSPLANTING (MID-APRIL)

1 Cut the root vertically using rooting scissors.

2 Scoop the roots downwards with a rake.

3 Cut the sides of the roots using rooting scissors.

※Akadama medium grain 80%; river sand 20%.

4 Prepare the pot and the soil for the bottom (akadama medium grain 80%, river sand 20%).

5 Add the soil, fix the tree and sprinkle with more soil.

6 Use tweezers to fill in any gaps in the soil.

7 Appearance after the transplanting is completed, with moss spread on the soil.

SPROUT CUTTING (EARLY JUNE)

1 Appearance when the sprouts are overgrown.

2 Use pruning scissors to cut the overgrown sprouts.

TIP

Similarly to vines, its sprouts grow very quickly, so sprout cutting should be done often.

3 Appearance after cutting is completed.

FERTILIZING (EARLY JUNE)

1 Fix four organic fertilizer stones around the verge of the pot.

2 Appearance after the fertilizing is completed.

TIP

If given too much fertilizer, the leaves won't turn red.

Moyogi, 6¾ in (17 cm) height, Ichiyou pot

Toukaede 唐楓

PROFILE

OTHER NAMES Japanese Trident Maple
CLASS Maple, Acer
TREE SHAPE Shakan, Moyogi, Kabutachi, Yoseue and others

With sprout plucking and leaf cutting, its branches give a delicate impression

Originally from China and Taiwan. The cycle of seasons looks wonderful on this tree. Being robust, it's very difficult to prune—excellent practice for beginners. The trick to dividing the branches well is to pluck sprouts and cut leaves often. When old, the bark comes off and the trunk becomes striped.

<table>
<tr><th>ACTION CALENDAR</th><th>Jan</th><th>Feb</th><th>Mar</th><th>Apr</th><th>May</th><th>Jun</th><th>Jul</th><th>Aug</th><th>Sep</th><th>Oct</th><th>Nov</th><th>Dec</th></tr>
<tr><td></td><td></td><td colspan="2">Transplanting</td><td></td><td colspan="3">Leaf cutting</td><td></td><td></td><td></td><td></td><td></td></tr>
<tr><td></td><td></td><td></td><td></td><td colspan="4">Sprout plucking</td><td></td><td></td><td></td><td></td><td></td></tr>
<tr><td></td><td></td><td></td><td></td><td></td><td colspan="3">Fertilizing</td><td></td><td colspan="3">Fertilizing</td><td></td></tr>
<tr><td></td><td colspan="3">Wire placing/ removal</td><td></td><td colspan="3">Wire placing/ removal</td><td></td><td colspan="4">Wire placing/ removal</td></tr>
</table>

MANAGEMENT TIPS

Placement Place under sunlight and in a well-ventilated spot. Move to shade during summer to avoid burning the leaves. Move under cover during winter.

Watering Give plenty of water when the soil dries. In summer, sprinkle the leaves in the evening.

Fertilizing Use solid fertilizer. If given too much fertilizer, the sprouts tend to overgrow, so moderate the amount according to the state of sprouts.

Pest Damage Be careful of white beetles, aphids, scale insects and powdery mildew.

Transplanting Transplant once every two years. Best time is between February and March.

TRANSPLANTING TO A SMALLER BOWL

Before: Late March

→

After: Late March

→

After: Mid-June

TRANSPLANTING (LATE MARCH)

1 Since the previous pot was significantly larger, roots should be significantly reduced and shortened.

TIP

By having smaller roots, the bonsai becomes weaker, making it easier to take care of.

2 Scoop the roots downwards with a rake.

3 Cut the longer roots using rooting scissors.

4 Appearance after cutting the longer roots. (Washing the roots)

5 Pour water into a bucket and wash the roots. Remove the moss with tweezers and rinse with water.

6 Find the main root and cut it with branch-cutting scissors. Also remove all unnecessary roots and leave only a few carefully chosen ones. (Cutting the main root)

7 Appearance after cutting the unnecessary roots.

8 If there are any roots sticking out to the sides, apply wire and lower them. (Correcting the roots)

9 Cut the thick roots with branch-cutting scissors. (Cutting the thick roots)

10 Appearance after cutting all thick roots.

11 Prepare the pot and the lower soil (80% akada-ma medium grain; 20% river sand. Add around 10% bamboo charcoal and into the mix).

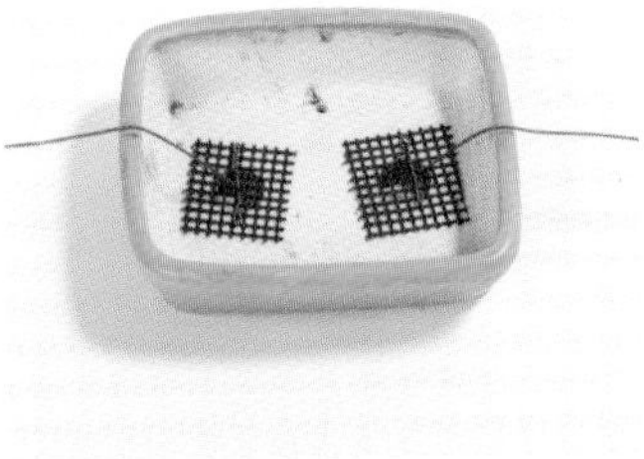

※Use 80% akadama medium grain; 20% river sand. Add around 10% worth of bamboo charcoal into the mix.

12 Appearance after transplanting is completed and moss is spread.

SPROUT PLUCKING (MID-MAY)

1 Trim the stems that have grown out.

LEAF CUTTING (MID-JUNE)

1 Appearance of the tree with overgrown leaves.

TIP

Reduce the amount to about ⅔ of the leaves.

2 Cut the leaves at their base with leaf-cutting scissors.

3 Appearance after leaf cutting is completed.

Shakan, 4¾ in (12 cm) height, basket pot

Nirekeyaki 楡欅

PROFILE

OTHER NAMES Akinire
CLASS Ulmaceae (deciduous tree)
TREE SHAPE Soukan, Moyogi and others

A tree that grows in a very short time! It's often recommended for beginners.

Originally from the western part of Honshu, this tree changes from green to yellow and withers depending on the season. The trunk grows thick very easily and the branches spread well, making the tree appear old in a short time. Often, cutting leaves will improve branching. Being very easy to raise even for beginners, it's a good choice among small bonsai.

MANAGEMENT TIPS

Placement Place the tree in a well-ventilated place with good sunlight. It can also grow in partial shade. Be careful of direct sunlight during summer, as it may cause the leaves to burn and wither.

Watering If you want to thicken the trunk, give plenty of water. Afterward you can adjust the amount of water based on the growth.

Fertilizing Give plenty of fertilizer, very often. If not given enough fertilizer, the branches might wither.

Pest Damage Be careful of aphids and beetles. Protect by applying insecticide.

Transplanting Due to its quick growth, transplant once a year. The best time is between March and April.

ACTIVITY CALENDAR

	Jan	Feb	Mar	Apr	May	Jun	Jul	Aug	Sep	Oct	Nov	Dec
Transplanting			■	■								
Sprout plucking/Leaf cutting				■	■	■	■	■	■			
Fertilizing						■	■		■	■	■	
Wire placing/ removal			■	■	■							

MAKING A MOYOGI

Before: Late March

→

After: Late March

→

After: Mid-June

PRUNING (LATE MARCH)

TIP

After cutting, apply a healing coating agent on the wound with a hard brush.

1 Cut unnecessary branches.

2 Appearance after pruning.

TRANSPLANTING (EARLY APRIL)

1 Move the roots downwards and scoop vertically with a rake.

2 Cut the longer roots using rooting scissors.

3 Appearance after the root cutting is finished.

4 Prepare the pot and the soil

※Akadama medium grain 80%; river sand 20%; also add 10% of bamboo charcoal into the mix.

TIP

Don't place the bamboo charcoal on the surface of the soil; it will float if you immerse the pot in water.

5 Place the soil, the tree and the top layer of soil.

※80% akadama small grain; 20% river sand.

6 Make sure there are no gaps by using tweezers or a bamboo skewer.

7 Appearance after transplanting is completed and moss is spread.

SPROUT CUTTING (MID-MAY)

1 Appearance of overgrown sprouts.

2 Use pruning shears to cut any sprouts sticking out past the tree's outline.

SPROUT CUTTING (MID-JUNE)

1 Appearance of overgrown sprouts.

2 Use pruning shears to cut the sprouts sticking out past the tree outline.

3 Appearance after sprout cutting is completed.

Hazenoki 黄櫨

Yoseue, 10 in (25 cm) height, Juetsu pot

PROFILE

OTHER NAMES Haze, Ryuukyuuhaze, Rounoki
CLASS Cashew
TREE SHAPE Yoseue, Moyogi, BunJingi, Ishitsuki and others

Beautiful crimson autumn leaves but be careful of rashes!

This grows in the western mountains of the Kanto region. The leaves have a beautiful gradient from green to red. Since it has a straight trunk and a small quantity of leaves, it's suitable for Yoseue. Despite being very robust, it gets dry very easily and requires frequent watering. When working on this species, always wear gloves to prevent rashes.

ACTION CALENDAR

Jan	Feb	Mar	Apr	May	Jun	Jul	Aug	Sep	Oct	Nov	Dec
		Transplanting									
					Leaf cutting	Leaf cutting					
				Fertilizing	Fertilizing						
		Wire placing/ removal	Wire placing/ removal								

MANAGEMENT TIPS

Placement Place in a well-ventilated, sunny place. If left in the shade, the branches' positioning will be haphazard.

Watering Be careful to not let it dry out. Adjust the amount of water based on the growth of the plant.

Fertilizing Give solid fertilizer. If given too much fertilizer, the red gradient of the leaves will be ruined.

Pest Damage Sprinkle fungicidal insecticide to avoid aphids.

Transplanting Transplant once a year. In the case of Yoseue, the roots might often fill the pot. The best time to transplant is March.

YOSEUE IN A SHALLOW POT (MULTIPLE TREES GROWING SIDE BY SIDE)

Before: Early November

→

Before: Early April

→

After: Early April

TRANSPLANTING (EARLY APRIL)

1 Scoop the roots downwards with a rake.

2 Clean the roots with an electric sprayer.

TIP

If you don't have an electric sprayer, you can use a water hose at very low pressure instead.

MEMO

Use gloves to prevent rashes and irritation

Especially when cutting the trunk, branches and roots, be careful of the sap. Always wear gloves when working on this tree.

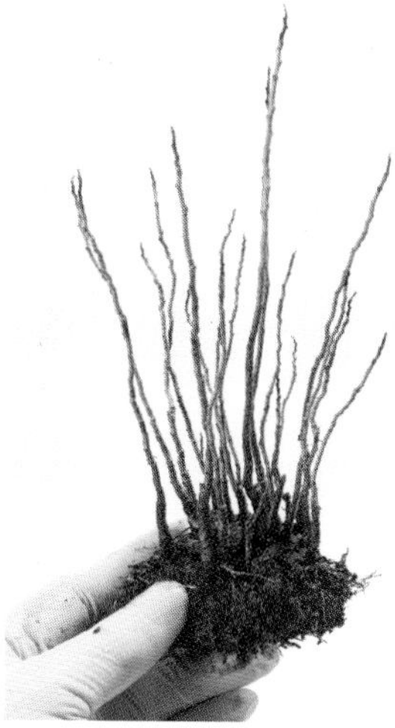

3 Appearance of clean roots.

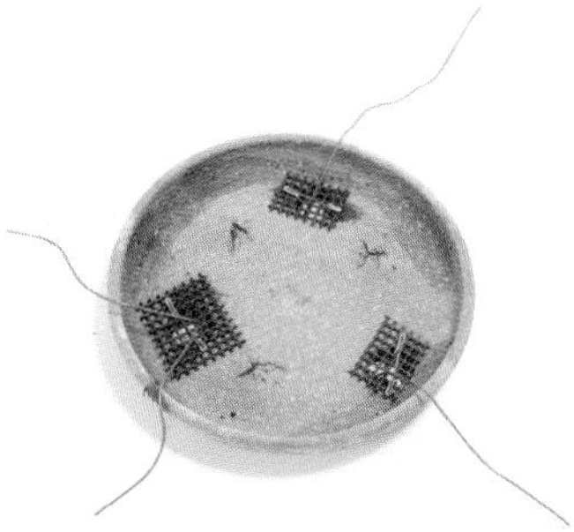

4 Prepare the pot and the soil (akadama medium grain 80%, river sand 20%).

※Use a mixture of akadama medium grain 80%; river sand 20%.

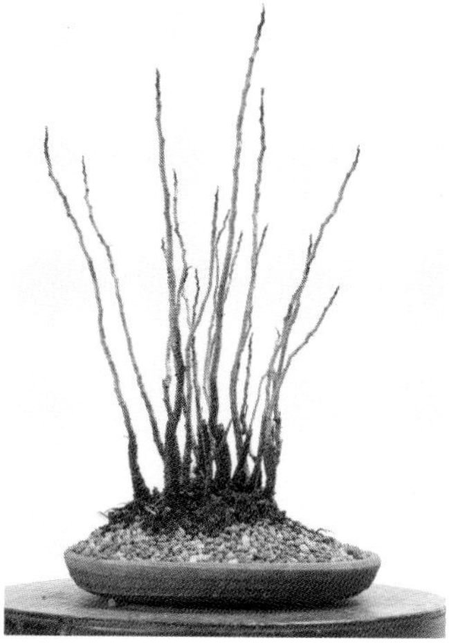

5 Appearance after the transplanting is completed.

PRUNING (EARLY APRIL)

1 Cut small unnecessary branches using pruning shears.

2 Appearance after pruning.

WIRING (EARLY APRIL)

1 Wrap one branch at a time and arrange them.

2 State after the wiring and arranging are completed.

3 Spread the moss.

4 Appearance when the new sprouts appear. (Mid-May)

Yoseue, 5½ in (14 cm) height, Hattori pot

Himeshara 姫沙羅

PROFILE

OTHER NAMES Stewartia
CLASS Theaceae
TREE SHAPE Shakan, Moyogi, Yoseue, Kabutachi and others

A trunk that changes color over time, from a pale light yellow to a reddish brown

A tree native to mountains, it is smaller in size than Nutsubaki and is suitable for bonsai. If planted as Yoseue, in about three years it'll look like a forest setting. What sets the bark apart is that, when young, it has a pale yellow color that will gradually grow darker and reddish with time. Leaves change typically with each season, and the tree has small white small white flowers similar to Tsubaki flowers.

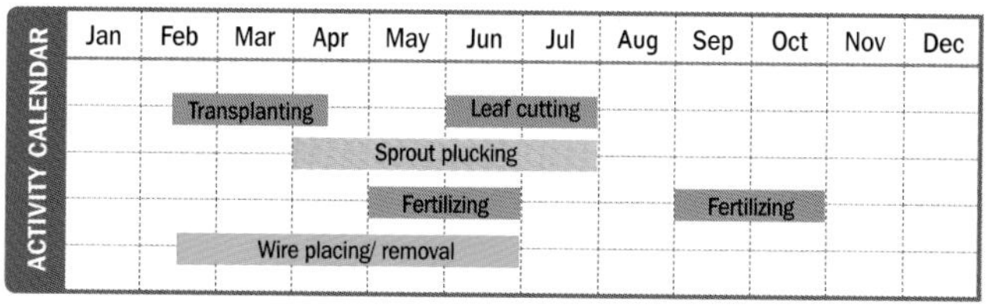

MANAGEMENT TIPS

Placement Place in shade or half-shade. During the summer keep in shade, move to partial shade during winter.

Watering Give plenty of water when the surface of the soil is dry. Giving too much water will result in overgrowth so be careful.

Fertilizing Use solid fertilizer. If too much fertilizer is given, the trunk will overgrow.

Pest Damage Be careful of scale insects. Provide good ventilation to avoid them.

Transplanting Once every two to three years. It is best done between mid-February and mid-April.

MAKING A YOSEUE

Before: Mid-February

→

After: Mid-February

→

After: Mid-June

PRUNING (MID-FEBRUARY)

1 Shorten the branches that were cut the previous year using pruning shears.

WIRING/BRANCH ARRANGING (MID-FEBRUARY)

1 Wrap one branch at a time.

TIP

To spread branches evenly, arrange branches one by one while keeping an eye on the balance of the branches.

2 Arrange the branches so that they're far spread.

3 Appearance after wiring and arranging are completed.

TRANSPLANTING (MID-FEBRUARY)

1 Prepare the pot.

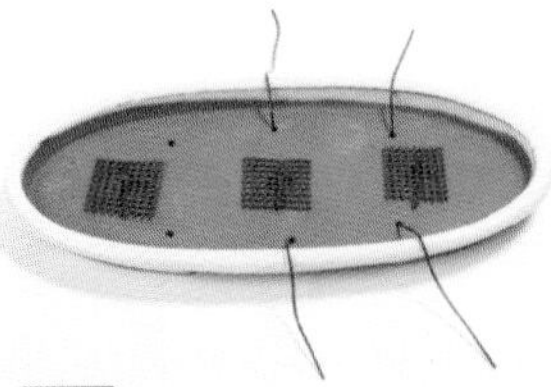

TIP

Since we will be planting on the right side, there is no need to wire the left side.

2 Scoop the soil away downwards with a rake and cut the roots on the sides using rooting scissors.

※Akadama medium grain.

3 Add soil and fix the tree on the right side.

4 Place and bend the wire with pliers on two points to fix the tree.

※Akadama small grain.

5 Add the rest of the soil (akadama small grain) and use tweezers to avoid any gaps on the surface.

6 Spray the surface with an electric high-pressure spray.

AFTER PLACING WATER MOSS, SPREAD MOSS (MID-FEBRUARY)

1 Lightly squeeze water-soaked water moss with your fingers and finely trim it using rooting scissors.

2 Spread water moss on the surface with tweezers.

3 Lightly press the water moss with your fingertips.

4 Keep lightly pressing the water moss while spritzing it to fix it to the ground.

5 Using pruning shears, cut the moss tips into small and fine pieces.

TIP

Since moss is easily blown away by water, it's a good idea to place the moss right after the water moss.

6 Grab the moss with the tip of the pruning shears and spread it on top of the water moss.

7 Lightly press the moss with your fingertips to fix it into place.

8 Spray the moss and the pot.

TIP

The reason we spray at this point is to clean the dirt around the pot and encourage the fusion of moss and the soil.

9 Appearance after the moss has been spread.

SPROUT CUTTING (MID-MAY)

1 Appearance of overgrown sprouts.

2 Use pruning shears to cut the sprouts sticking out past the tree outline.

3 Appearance after sprout cutting is finished.

SPROUT CUTTING (MID-JUNE)

1 Use pruning shears to cut the sprouts sticking out past the tree outline.

2 Appearance after sprout cutting is finished.

Yoseue, 9 in (23 cm) height, Hattori pot

Buna 山毛欅

PROFILE

OTHER NAMES Yuzuriha
CLASS Fagaceae
TREE SHAPE Chokkan, Shakan, Moyogi, Kabutachi, Yoseue and others

A shiny white bark and color-changing leaves

When growing in the mountain forests, the leaves and trunk of this tree vary depending on the location of its growth. When grown as bonsai, their trunk grows whitish in color over time. Flowers and fresh leaves appear around May.

ACTION CALENDAR

<table>
<tr><th>Jan</th><th>Feb</th><th>Mar</th><th>Apr</th><th>May</th><th>Jun</th><th>Jul</th><th>Aug</th><th>Sep</th><th>Oct</th><th>Nov</th><th>Dec</th></tr>
<tr><td></td><td></td><td colspan="2">Transplanting</td><td></td><td colspan="2">Leaf cutting</td><td></td><td></td><td></td><td></td><td></td></tr>
<tr><td></td><td></td><td></td><td colspan="2">Sprout plucking</td><td></td><td></td><td></td><td></td><td></td><td></td><td></td></tr>
<tr><td></td><td></td><td></td><td></td><td colspan="2">Fertilizing</td><td></td><td></td><td colspan="2">Fertilizing</td><td></td><td></td></tr>
<tr><td colspan="6">Wire placing/ removal</td><td></td><td></td><td></td><td></td><td></td><td>Wire placing/ removal</td></tr>
</table>

MANAGEMENT TIPS

Placement	Place in a well-lit, well-ventilated place. In summer, protect it with a cheesecloth. In winter move it under cover.
Watering	It likes water. Be careful to not let it dry out during summer. Water the leaves in summer evenings.
Fertilizing	Give solid fertilizer. Be careful of giving too much, since excessive fertilizing distorts the tree shape.
Pest Damage	Be careful of aphids and scale insects.
Transplanting	Once every two years. Best time is between March and April.

MAKING A BUNJINGI

Before: Early April

→

After: Early April

→

After: Mid-May

PRUNING (EARLY APRIL)

1 Use tweezers to pick the sprouts located on the base of the branches.

TIP

If those sprouts are left on their own, they'll quickly grow thick, so it's important to pick them early.

WIRING/BRANCH ARRANGING (EARLY APRIL)

1 Cut small unnecessary branches using pruning shears.

2 Appearance after pruning.

TRANSPLANTING (EARLY APRIL)

1 Scoop the roots downwards with a rake then cut the longer roots using rooting scissors.

2 Prepare the pot and soil.

※Akadama medium 80%, river sand 20%.

3 Appearance after the transplanting is completed and moss has been spread.

Momiji 紅葉

PROFILE

OTHER NAMES Kaede
CLASS Maple
TREE SHAPE Moyogi, Kabutachi, Kengai, Yoseue, Ishitsuk

Yamamomiji, Moyogi, 7 in (18 cm) height, yellow glazed round pot

A true representative of Japanese trees, a sight for every season

In the bonsai world, if the leaves have more than five fissures the tree is called "Momiji;" if they have three, the tree is called "Kaede." When made into a bonsai the Yamamomiji is robust and easy to grow. Its variety makes it enjoyable in every season. There are also many different species, with blue varieties being fairly popular.

MANAGEMENT TIPS

Placement Place in a well-lit and well-ventilated spot. In summer, use a cheese cloth to protect the tree. In winter place under cover in a well-lit spot.

Watering When the surface of the soil is dry, give plenty of water. Be careful to not let it dry out during summer. Water the leaves in summer evenings.

Fertilizing Give solid fertilizer. Be careful of giving too much, as over fertilizing thickens the branches excessively.

Pest Damage Be careful of aphids and powdery mildew. Hang the leaves and provide good ventilation for the tree.

Transplanting Once every two to three years. Ideal time is between February and March.

Aoshidare Momiji, Hankengai, 10¼ in (26 cm) height, 15 in (38 cm) width, victory pot.

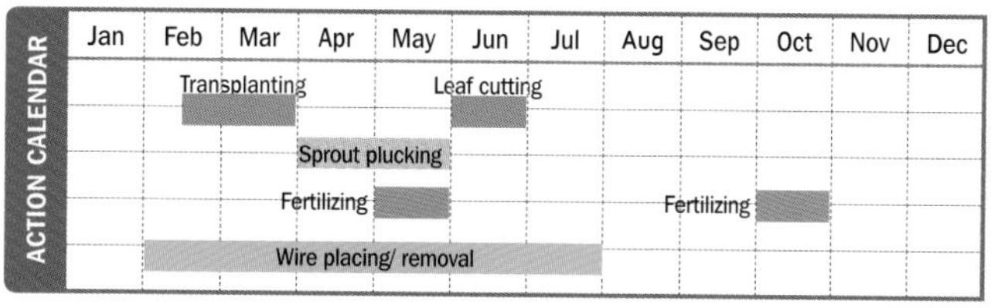

CHANGING THE TREE SHAPE

Before: Mid-April

→

After: Mid-April

SPROUT PLUCKING (MID-APRIL)

1 Pluck the tip of the overgrown sprouts with tweezers.

TIP

We'll make these our "main" branches. Wire them all the way to the tip and let them grow long.

2 Pluck also the small sprouts.

WIRING/BRANCH ARRANGING (MID-APRIL)

TIP

We do this during the spring. Since the branches are straight at this point, bend and arrange them slightly through wiring.

1 Wrap one branch at a time.

TIP

When the sprouts start growing again, pluck and wire again. This should be done three or four times in the spring.

2 Arrange the branches so that they're far spread.

MAKING A SHAKAN (DIAGONAL BONSAI)

Before: Early April

After: Early April

PRUNING (EARLY APRIL)

1 When the branches start to look too crowded, prune them using pruning shears.

2 Appearance after pruning is completed.

TREATING WOUNDS (EARLY APRIL)

1 If there's a large cut, carve it with a carving knife.

2 Apply India Ink (also known as China Ink) on the wound.

TIP

In the case of the Momiji, if the usual healing agent is applied, instead of healing, the cut will form into a hump, and it will be necessary to carve it again.

WIRING (LATE APRIL)

1 Wrap one branch at a time and arrange the branches with their tips aiming downward.

2 Appearance after the wiring and arranging are completed.

TRANSPLANTING (LATE APRIL)

※From the second transplant onwards, transplant between February and March.

1 Cut the upper part of the roots using rooting scissors.

2 Cut the sides of the roots using rooting scissors.

3 Appearance after cutting the roots.

4 Prepare the pot and the soil.

※Akadama medium 80%; river sand 20%.

5 Place the tree and the top layer of soil (akadama small 80%; river sand 20%).

※Akadama small 80%; river sand 20%.

6 Use tweezers to make sure there are no gaps in the soil.

7 Appearance after transplanting is completed and moss had been spread.

SPROUT CUTTING (MID-MAY)

1 Appearance of grown new sprouts.

2 Use pruning scissors to cut the grown sprouts.

WIRING (MID-MAY)

1 Wrap the new sprouts in wire.

2 Appearance after the wiring and arranging are completed.

LEAF TRIMMING (LATE JUNE)

1 Appearance of grown leaves.

2 Cut the leaves off just a little bit past their base.

3 Appearance after leaf cutting is completed.

Kabutachi, 8½ in (21 cm) height, Silent Japanese pot

Asebi 馬酔木

PROFILE

OTHER NAMES Asebo
CLASS Ericaceae
TREE SHAPE Kabutachi

Pretty bell-shaped flowers blooming in tufts

Originally both a Japanese and Himalayan species. The leaves and stems contain a toxic substance—it's said that in ancient times, eating this plant caused horses to hallucinate. The leaves do not fall in winter. The flowers have a similar shape to Dudantsutuji, and can be red, peach and white in color.

ACTION CALENDAR

Jan	Feb	Mar	Apr	May	Jun	Jul	Aug	Sep	Oct	Nov	Dec
		Transplanting	Transplanting					Transplanting	Transplanting		
			Fertilizing	Fertilizing	Fertilizing			Fertilizing	Fertilizing		
					Wire placing/ removal						

MANAGEMENT TIPS

Placement Place in a well-lit and well-ventilated spot. It can also grow in partial shade, but that will negatively affect the flowers.

Watering In the growth period between spring to fall give plenty of water.

Fertilizing Use solid fertilizer.

Pest Damage Be careful of tree bugs and moths.

Transplanting Once every two years. Best time is between March and mid-April.

TRANSPLANTING TO A COLORED POT

Before: Late March

→

After: Late March

PRUNING (LATE MARCH)

1 Use pruning shears to cut small deformed branches.

2 Also cut the unnecessary branches.

3 Appearance after pruning is completed.

TRANSPLANTING (LATE MARCH)

1 Appearance after we used a rake to scoop the roots downwards, then cut the long roots using rooting scissors.

※Use a mixture of 80% akadama medium grain, 20% river sand, and add about 10% bamboo charcoal.

2 Prepare the pot with the soil (akadama medium 80%; river sand 20%, Add around 10% worth of bamboo charcoal to the mix).

TIP

Don't place the bamboo charcoal on the surface of the soil since it will float if you immerse the pot in water.

3 Place the tree and the top layer of soil (akadama small 80%; river sand 20%).

4 Appearance after transplanting is completed and moss has been spread.

MEMO

Tip for better flowers

Flowers bloom from the tip of new sprouts. In order to keep the outline of the tree shape, cut only overgrown branches and don't cut them again.

Iwagarami 岩絡

PROFILE

OTHER NAMES Japanese Hydrangea
CLASS Saxifrages
TREE SHAPE Shakan, Moyogi, Kengai

Hankengai, 5¼ in (13 cm) height, 8 in (20 cm) width, Japanese pot

Flowers bloom in mid-June

It grows entwined to rocks and trees with fresh white blooming flowers

This grows in the mountains of Japan, usually entwining itself around stones and trees, spreading by growing new roots from stalks. Despite being a vine species, it makes a good bonsai and is actually pretty easy to grow. Trunk cutting and root hiding can also be done. In June, it grows small, white flowers similar to Hydrangea.

ACTION CALENDAR

Jan	Feb	Mar	Apr	May	Jun	Jul	Aug	Sep	Oct	Nov	Dec
		Transplanting			Leaf cutting						
			Sprout plucking								
				Fertilizing				Fertilizing			
			Wire placing/ removal								

MANAGEMENT TIPS

Placement Place in a well-lit spot. In summer, to avoid leaf burning, move it to partial shade. In winter, move under cover.

Watering Give a lot of water. It likes humid air. In summer evenings, water the leaves too.

Fertilizing Use solid fertilizer.

Pest Damage It's mostly safe from pest damage.

Transplanting Once every two years. Ideal time is between March and April.

MAKING A HANKENGAI

Before: Early April

→

Before: Early November

→

After: Early April

→

After: Late April

WIRING (EARLY APRIL)

1 Wrap one branch at a time and arrange the branches.

2 Appearance after the wiring and arranging are completed.

TRANSPLANTING (EARLY APRIL)

1 Use a rake to scoop the roots downwards vertically.

2 Appearance after scooping.

3 Prepare the pot and the soil (akadama medium 80%; river sand 20%).

※Use a mixture of 80% akadama medium grain, 20% river sand.

4 Appearance after transplanting is completed and moss has been spread.

MEMO

Tip for better flowers

In summer, leave the tree in partial shade. If the leaves burn, nutrients are lost, causing the flowers to grow misshapen.

Ume 梅

Kengai, 12 in (30 cm) height, 22 in (56 cm),
Namako glazed pot

PROFILE

OTHER NAMES Japanese plum
CLASS Rosaceae, Prunus (deciduous tree)
TREE SHAPE Moyogi, Shakan, BunJingi, Hankengai

Contrast between heavy stems of an old tree and pretty young flowers

Originally from China, this tree's flowers have been appreciated since ancient times. It blooms in late winter. The combination of beautiful fresh blossoms with the tree's overall look of antiquity is what makes this bonsai universally loved. Cut the branches soon after the flower season but be careful to not cut the new sprouts.

ACTION CALENDAR

Jan	Feb	Mar	Apr	May	Jun	Jul	Aug	Sep	Oct	Nov	Dec
	Transplanting							Transplanting			
			Fertilizing					Fertilizing			
	Wire placing/ removal										

MANAGEMENT TIPS

Placement Place in a well-lit and well-ventilated spot.

Watering When the surface of the soil is dry, give plenty of water. For growing flowers, let the soil dry slightly between June and August.

Fertilizing Use solid fertilizer.

Pest Damage Be careful of aphids, scale insects and black spots.

Transplanting Once every two to three years. Best time is either between February to March or September to October.

TRANSPLANTING TO A BONSAI POT

Before: Mid-February

After: Mid-February

After: Late June

FLOWER PLUCKING (MID-FEBRUARY)

1 Remove 70–80% of the open flowers.

PRUNING (MID-FEBRUARY)

TIP

The reason we cut tall branches is in order to reduce the tree's height.

1 Cut unnecessary branches and the tip of all other branches using pruning scissors.

2 Cut old wounded branches (previously cut) with branch-cutting scissors again.

WIRING/ARRANGING (MID-FEBRUARY)

TIP

For the Ume, don't force the branches to bend, as they will break.

1 Wrap one branch at a time and arrange the branches.

2 Appearance after the wiring and arranging are completed.

3 On cut wounds, apply healing agent with a hard brush.

TRANSPLANTING (MID-FEBRUARY)

1 Use a rake to scoop the upper part of the roots.

2 Use a rake to scoop the lower part of the roots.

3 Appearance after scooping.

4 Cut the longer roots using rooting scissors.

5 Appearance after cutting.

6 Clean the roots with a toothbrush.

TIP

We clean the base of the tree because after replanting, a major section that was previously under the soil will be visible.

7 Prepare the pot and the lower soil (80% akadama medium grain; 20% river sand. Add around 10% worth of bamboo charcoal into the mix).

※Use a mixture of 80% akadama medium grain, 20% river sand, and add about 10% bamboo charcoal.

8 Place the soil and the tree, and cover with the top layer of soil (80% akadama small grain; 20% river sand).

Don't place the bamboo charcoal on the surface of the soil; it will float if you immerse the pot in water.

※Use a mixture of 80% akadama small grain, 20% river sand.

9 Using tweezers or a bamboo skewer, make sure there are no gaps in the soil.

10 Bend the wire in a single spot and fix the tree.

11 Cut the excess wire with wire cutters.

12 Place more soil on top after fixing the tree. (80% akadama small grain; 20% river sand).

※Use a mixture of 80% akadama small grain, 20% river sand.

13 Fill a bucket with water and immerse the pot so that the water level is aligned with the top of the soil. Keep in water until the soil is fully soaked.

14 Appearance after the transplanting is completed and moss has been spread.

CUTTING THE LEAVES AT THE BASE OF BRANCHES (EARLY JUNE)

1 Appearance of the tree after it's grown.

TIP

This is a peculiar activity performed only on Ume. Since it's rare for new sprouts to appear after the flowers bloom, we do this to make sure that new sprouts can grow without affecting the flowers.

2 Cut the two leaves at the base of each branch with leaf-cutting scissors.

WIRING (EARLY JUNE)

TIP

Since Ume branches are usually straight, at most you can just bend them a little bit.

1 Wrap one branch at a time and arrange the branches.

2 Appearance after the wiring and arranging are completed.

※Tip for Hanamono: If you pluck the very tip of new sprouts they'll grow longer. New sprouts usually appear around April. When the branches spread from one to five or six, the flowers will bloom in June or July.

Shakan, 10 in (25 cm) height, Chinese pot

Kibushi 木五倍子

PROFILE

OTHER NAMES Kifushi
CLASS Stachyuraceae
TREE SHAPE Moyogi, BunJingi, Kengai and others

Pale yellow flowers hang from branches, heralding the start of spring

Native to Japan, this bonsai is robust and easy for beginners to grow. In fall, the bright petals drop, growing again in early spring. It's a hermaphrodite species, with female flowers that are 2¾–3¼ in (7–8 cm) long. In addition to the beautiful flowers, the cycle of seasons is lovely to behold.

ACTION CALENDAR

	Jan	Feb	Mar	Apr	May	Jun	Jul	Aug	Sep	Oct	Nov	Dec
Transplanting			■									
Sprout plucking				■								
Fertilizing				■	■	■			■	■		
Wire placing/ removal	■	■	■	■	■	■						■

MANAGEMENT TIPS

Placement Place in a well-lit and well-ventilated area. In summer, avoid direct sunlight in the afternoon. In winter move the tree under cover.

Watering It likes water. When the surface of the soil is dry, give plenty of water. In case of a deep pot, soaking is suggested in the summer.

Fertilizing Use solid fertilizer.

Pest Damage Be careful of scale insects.

Transplanting Once every 1–2 years. Best time is in March.

CHANGING THE TREE SHAPE

Before: Mid-November

→

Before: Early March

→

After: Early March

→

After: Mid-June

WOUND TREATMENT (EARLY MARCH)

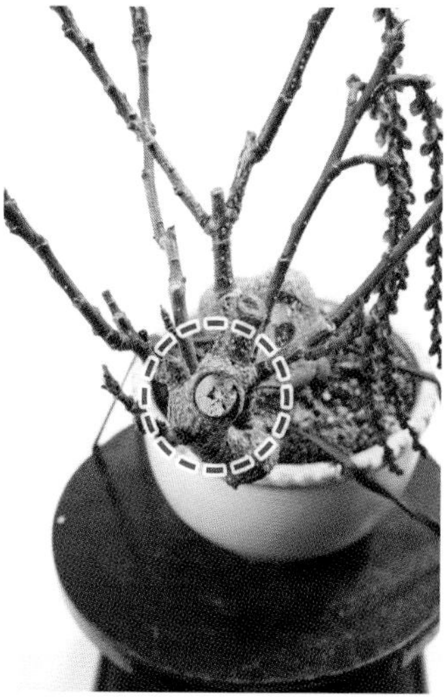

1 In this case, there's an old wound on the tree.

2 Carve the wound with a carving knife.

TIP

Perform the next step immediately after carving on the wound. Leaving it untreated may cause the wound to rot.

3 Apply a healing agent on the cut with a hard brush.

WIRING (LATE MARCH)

1 Wrap one branch at a time and arrange the branches.

2 Appearance after the wiring and arranging are completed and moss has been spread.

MEMO

Tip for better flowers

Pluck the tip of new sprouts and give solid fertilizer (use specific fertilizer rich in phosphoric acid and potassium). In mid-June the next year's flower sprouts will start growing.

Flowering is in early June

Kinrobai 金露梅

PROFILE

OTHER NAMES *Potentilla fruticosa*
CLASS Rosaceae, Dasiphora (deciduous shrub)
TREE SHAPE Moyogi, Kabutachi, Kengai

Ume-like flowers with bright and vivid colors

Originally from the Northern Hemisphere. The flower shape is similar to Ume. It's often cultivated in gardening, and has a fair number of varieties. The buds go from yellow to white, transitioning to a peach color. About a month after that, the flowers bloom. If brushed after the leaves have fallen, the tree it will have a glossy look.

Moyogi, 6 in (15 cm) height, Iwai pot

ACTION CALENDAR

Jan	Feb	Mar	Apr	May	Jun	Jul	Aug	Sep	Oct	Nov	Dec
Transplanting							Transplanting				
			Sprout plucking								
			Fertilizing					Fertilizing			
Wire placing/ removal				Wire placing/ removal							

MANAGEMENT TIPS

Placement Place in a well-lit and well-ventilated spot. It resists cold and can also stand up to being covered in snow.

Watering When the surface of the soil is dry, give plenty of water. Be careful of roots rotting due to excessive humidity during summer.

Fertilizing Give solid fertilizer.

Pest Damage Be careful of aphids and snout moths.

Transplanting Once every two years. The best time is either March or October.

TRANSPLANTING TO A POT THAT MATCHES THE TREE

Before: Late March

→

After: Late March

→

After: Mid-May

CLEANING BARK AND BRANCHES (LATE MARCH)

1 Use a wire brush to clean the old bark.

2 Appearance after cleaning.

3 Use a high water pressure washer (using a hose and narrowing the tip also works) to clean part of the trunk.

4 Appearance after washing.

TRANSPLANTING (LATE MARCH)

1 Cut the sides of the roots using rooting scissors.

2 Appearance after the cutting is completed.

3 Prepare the pot and the lower soil (akadama medium 80%; river sand 20%; add about 10% worth of bamboo charcoal into the mix).

※Use a mixture of 80% akadama medium grain, 20% river sand, and add about 10% bamboo charcoal.

4 Appearance after the transplanting is completed and moss has been spread.

※Tip for better flowers: Pluck the tip of new sprouts. Give plenty of solid fertilizer (use specific fertilizer rich in phosphoric acid and potassium) in April before the flowers start appearing.

Oshidori Sakura, Moyogi, 10 in (25 cm) height, Mortar pot

Juugatsuzakura (October Sakura)

Unryuuzakura (dynasty Sakura)

Sakura 桜

PROFILE

OTHER NAMES Japanese cherry
CLASS Rosaceae, Prunus (deciduous tree)
TREE SHAPE Moyogi, Shakan, BunJing

The symbol of spring in Japan with its gorgeous flowers!

Sakura is loved all over the world, and there are about 200 different varieties symbolizing spring in Japan. The Oshidori Sakura pictured here (also called the Fuji Cherry) has double flowers. When used in bonsai, the most important feature is its look of antiquity. Let branches grow in any direction and also let them grow fairly long.

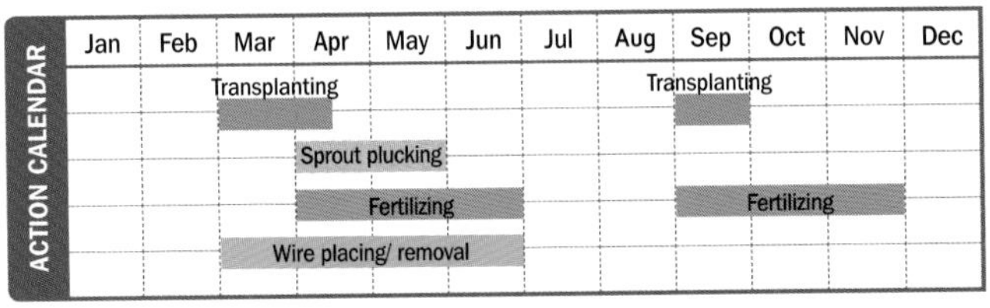

MANAGEMENT TIPS

Placement Place in a well-lit and well-ventilated area. In summer, avoid direct sunlight in the afternoon. In winter move the tree under the cover.

Watering It's very vulnerable to drying. If left without water it takes a long time to recover; however, giving too much water will ruin the flowers.

Fertilizing Use solid fertilizer.

Pest Damage Be careful of aphids, caterpillars, scale insects and root carcinoma.

Transplanting Once every two years. Best time is between late March and mid-April or in September.

SHAPING THE TREE INTO BEING A FUKINAGASHI (WINDSOCK SHAPE)

Before: Early March

→

After: Early March

WIRING (EARLY MARCH)

1 Wrap one branch at a time and arrange the branches.

TIP

By bending we make the tree shape more elegant.

2 Bend the branches that are straight.

3 Appearance after the wiring and arranging are completed and moss has been applied.

TRANSPLANTING (EARLY MARCH)

TIP

Cutting the roots first makes it easier to scoop them later.

1 Cut the roots vertically using rooting scissors.

2 Scoop the roots downwards with a rake.

3 Cut the longer roots using rooting scissors.

4 Appearance after cutting.

5 Prepare the pot and the lower soil (80% akadama medium grain; 20% river sand. Add around 10% worth of bamboo charcoal into the mix).

※Use a mixture of 80% akadama medium grain, 20% river sand, and add about 10% bamboo charcoal.

6 Place the soil and the tree, and fix the tree with wire on one point.

TIP

Don't place the bamboo charcoal on the surface of the soil; it will float if you immerse the pot in water.

7 Place the top layer of soil (80% akadama small grain; 20% river sand).

※Use a mixture of 80% akadama small grain, 20% river sand.

8 Make sure there are no gaps, using tweezers or a bamboo skewer.

9 Appearance after transplanting is completed and the moss has been spread.

WIRING/BRANCH ARRANGING (MID-MAY)

1 Appearance of grown sprouts.

2 Wrap wire around the top of the tree and bend it.

TIP

The appearance of low branches calms down the viewer and it also has the effect of increasing the spread of the flowers.

TIP

Until next year's flowers start sprouting, leave the wiring untouched. From fall to spring, give plenty of fertilizer.

3 Appearance after wiring and branch arranging are completed.

MEMO

Tips for better flowers

1. If the Sakura is pruned too short, it won't produce flowers. If a branch has more than five leaves, prune the branch from the fifth leaf.
2. Try to avoid cutting the leaves.
3. If given too much fertilizer, it'll sprout a second time without producing flowers.

Moyogi, 5¼ in (13 cm) height, celebration pot

Zakuro 石榴

PROFILE

OTHER NAMES Pomegranate, Jakuro
CLASS Lythraceae, Punica (deciduous tree)
TREE SHAPE Moyogi, Hankengai

The strength of a twisted trunk with bright flowers

Originally from the Middle East and Mediterranean, this much-appreciated tree changes from season to season. The trunk has a beautiful natural twist. The younger species also have charming fruit varieties. When buying, look for one with a thick trunk.

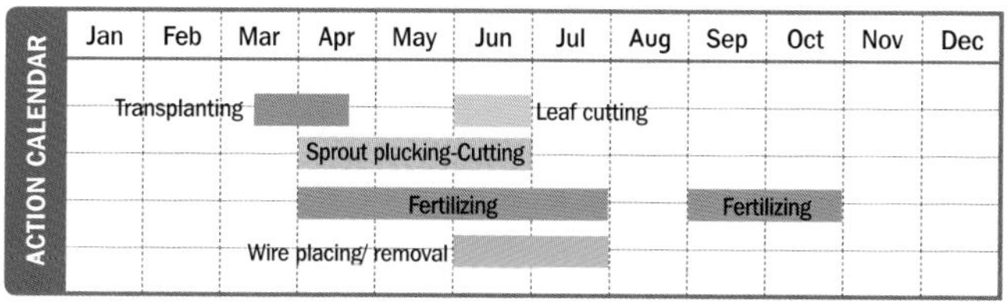

MANAGEMENT TIPS

Placement Place in a well-lit and well-ventilated area. During summer avoid late afternoon sunlight. During winter move it under the cover.

Watering Let it be a little dry. If it's too moist, it could suffer from root rot.

Fertilizing Use solid fertilizer.

Pest Damage Be careful of aphids, scale insects, thrips and beetles.

Transplanting Once every two years. Best time is between mid-March and mid-April.

TRANSPLANTING INTO A FLAT POT

Before: Late March

After: Late March

After: Early June

TRANSPLANTING (LATE MARCH)

1 Place the tree in a draining basket/colander and trim any roots that stick out.

TIP

By placing the tree in a colander, we avoid bending and pushing the roots together.

2 Scoop the roots downwards with a rake, then cut the longer roots. This is the appearance after this step is completed.

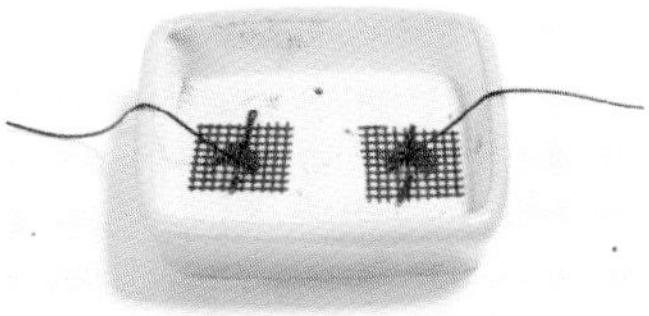

3 Prepare the pot and the soil (80% akadama medium grain; 20% river sand. Add around 10% worth of bamboo charcoal into the mix).

※Use a mixture of 80% akadama medium grain, 20% river sand, and add about 10% bamboo charcoal.

4 Appearance after transplanting is completed, and moss has been spread.

SPROUT PLUCKING (MID-MAY)

1 Appearance of grown sprouts.

2 Cut the overgrown sprouts with leaf-cutting scissors.

SPROUT CUTTING (EARLY JUNE)

1 Prune grown sprouts using pruning shears.

2 Appearance after sprouts have been cut.

※Tip for better flowers: Pluck the tip of new sprouts and give fertilizers that are rich in phosphoric acid and potassium.

Satsuki 皐月

PROFILE

OTHER NAMES Satsuki tsutsuji
CLASS Ericaceae, Rhododendron (evergreen shrub)
TREE SHAPE Chokkan, Soukan, BunJingi, Kengai, Yoseue

Matsunami Satsuki; Moyogi, 8 in (20 cm) height, Japanese styled pot

Extremely popular for their large variety of flowers

Originally from western Kanto and southern Kyushu. These trees grow on rocks near water sources. Flowers can be either single or double. The colors are very saturated and there are more than a thousand varieties. It resists artificial cutting, but its trunk thickens easily, making it easy to shape as desired. In the case of the Matsunami variety, shown here, flowers bloom and spread in March–April.

MANAGEMENT TIPS

Placement Place in a well-lit and well-ventilated area. In summer, avoid direct sunlight in the afternoon. In winter move the tree under the cover.

Watering It likes water; don't let it dry out.

Fertilizing Use solid fertilizer.

Pest Damage Be careful of tingidae. If the leaves' color starts to fade, apply treatment.

Transplanting Once every two years. It can be done in March or in late June.

ACTION CALENDAR

Jan	Feb	Mar	Apr	May	Jun	Jul	Aug	Sep	Oct	Nov	Dec
		Transplanting			Transplanting						
					Sprout plucking	Sprout plucking					
			Fertilizing		Fertilizing			Fertilizing	Fertilizing		
	Wire placing/removal	Wire placing/removal				Wire placing/removal	Wire placing/removal				

MAKING A MOYOGI

Before: Mid-February

→

After: Mid-February

→

After: Mid-June

PRUNING (MID-FEBRUARY)

1 Cut the root of the branches using pruning scissors.

2 Make the cut section flat.

3 Appearance after pruning.

4 Apply healing coating agent with a hard brush on the cuts.

WIRING/BRANCH ARRANGING (MID-FEBRUARY)

1 Wrap one branch at a time and arrange them.

2 Appearance after wiring and branch arrangement are completed.

TRANSPLANTING (MID-FEBRUARY)

※For the following transplant, alternate to March.

TIP

Satsuki roots are fine and hard to work with, so use rooting scissors for this step to avoid any damage.

1 Scoop and loosen the roots with a rake, then cut the roots in a vertical V shape using rooting scissors.

2 Appearance after the root cutting.

3 Prepare the pot and the soil (akadama medium grain) then plant the tree.

4 Use a hard brush or some tweezers to make sure there are no gaps in the soil.

SPREADING THE WATER MOSS (MID-FEBRUARY)

1 Soak the water moss in water and shape it into a string-like shape.

2 Place it on the base of the roots while gently pressing on it to fix it to the soil.

3 Shape some wire in a U shape and use it to fix the water moss.

4 Appearance after moss is spread.

PRUNING (LATE APRIL)

1 Appearance of new sprouts.

2 Use pruning scissors to prune the new sprouts.

TIP

Cutting the new sprouts will cause an increase in the number of branches.

3 Appearance after pruning.

SPROUT PLUCKING (MID-JUNE)

1 Appearance of grown sprouts.

2 From the trunk some extra sprouts will appear, defined as "indecisive sprouts."

TIP

In the case of Satsuki, if cut immediately, these small sprouts will not leave any mark on the tree.

3 Use tweezers to pluck out the "indecisive sprouts."

4 Also pluck out overgrown sprouts.

5 Appearance after plucking is completed.

※Tip: To help improve flower health, disinfect the tree with insecticide or disinfectant. Spray twice a month between June and November.

Sanshuyu 山茱萸

PROFILE

OTHER NAMES Haruko Ganebana, Akisango
CLASS Cornaceae, Cornus (dogwood)
TREE SHAPE Moyogi, Kabudachi

Moyogi, 6¾ in (17 cm) height, eastern pot

Small golden flowers shine and spread during spring

Originally from China and Korea. The tree has yellow flowers in early spring; in the fall it grows an elliptical red fruit commonly called "the fall coral" in Japan. Being robust, it resists being artificially cut. Even when its branches are very fine, it makes an impressive appearance.

In early March, we wire the branches one by one and arrange them.

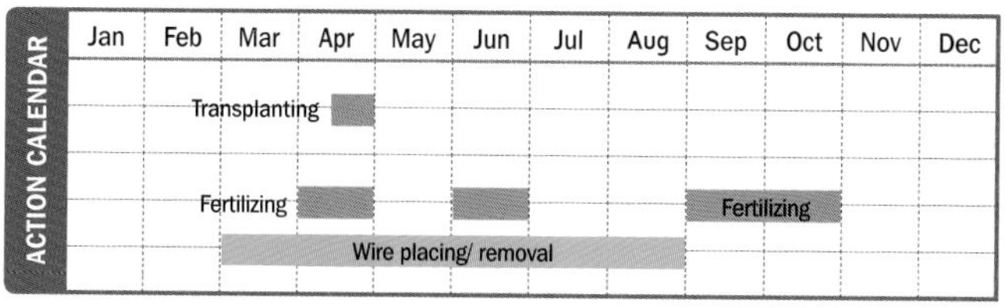

MANAGEMENT TIPS

Placement	Place in a well-lit and well-ventilated area.
Watering	Whenever the surface of the soil is dry, give plenty of water. Be careful to not let it dry out.
Fertilizing	Use solid fertilizer for Hanamono (rich in phosphoric acid and potassium).
Pest Damage	Be careful of *Parasa consocia* (moth).
Transplanting	Once every two years. Transplant in mid-April.

CHANGING THE POT ACCORDING TO THE COLOR OF THE FLOWERS

Before: Early November

→

Before: Early March

→

After: Early March

CHANOKI 茶

Kengai, 7 in (18 cm) height, 10¼ in (26 cm) width, Chinese pot

PROFILE

OTHER NAMES Tea plant
CLASS Theaceae, Camellia (evergreen)
TREE SHAPE Kengai, Kabutachi, Shakan

Large round white flowers and a balance in the number of flowers

Originally from China. Leaves can be processed into green tea, Oolong and more. The bright yellow stamens on the round white petals have strong visual impact. In the case of bonsai, the trick to keeping the amount of flowering low is to keep the balance of the growth in mind. As this species is weak to cold, it should be transplanted only during warmer periods.

ACTION CALENDAR

	Jan	Feb	Mar	Apr	May	Jun	Jul	Aug	Sep	Oct	Nov	Dec
Transplanting			■	■								
Sprout plucking				■	■	■	■	■	■			
Fertilizing				■	■	■	■	■	■			
Wire placing/ removal			■	■	■	■	■					

MANAGEMENT TIPS

Placement Place the tree in a well-ventilated place with good sunlight. When new sprouts emerge, be careful of late spring frost.

Watering Water generously when the surface of the soil is dry.

Fertilizing Give plenty of solid fertilizer.

Pest Damage Be careful of white root-rot and larvae.

Transplanting Once every two years. Best time is between mid-March and mid-April.

PREPARING A KENGAI

Before: Mid-April

→

After: Mid-April

→

After: Mid-May

LEAF CUTTING (MID-APRIL)

TIP

We cut the leaves because it's an evergreen tree. Since usually the leaves on the upper side are stronger, we also cut leaves so that sprouts will emerge uniformly on lower branches as well.

1 Cut leaves at their base with leaf-cutting scissors.

2 Appearance after the leaf cutting is completed.

WIRING (MID-APRIL)

1 Wrap one branch at a time and arrange the branches.

2 Appearance after the wiring and arranging are completed.

TRANSPLANTING (MID-APRIL)

1 Scoop the roots downwards with a rake then cut the longer roots using rooting scissors.

2 Appearance after transplanting is completed and the moss has been spread.

※Use akadama medium grain 80%/ river sand 20% for the soil.
※Tip for better flowers: Pluck the tip of new sprouts.
Use phosphoric acid and potassium rich fertilizer.

Chojubai 長寿梅

PROFILE

OTHER NAMES Boke
CLASS Rosaceae
TREE SHAPE Shakan, Moyogi, Kabutachi, Kengai, Ishitsuki

Moyogi, 6¾ in (17 cm) height, moon scallion round pot

Beautiful flowers in every season combined with an ancient look

Originally from Japan, it's said to be a variant of Kusaboke. It has beautiful flowers in each season of the year. As it blooms during winter, it's often shown at winter exhibitions. In the case of the bonsai variant, flowers are red or white. Branches are dense and finely separated, so it's easy to grow this tree, even for beginners.

ACTION CALENDAR

<table>
<tr><th>Jan</th><th>Feb</th><th>Mar</th><th>Apr</th><th>May</th><th>Jun</th><th>Jul</th><th>Aug</th><th>Sep</th><th>Oct</th><th>Nov</th><th>Dec</th></tr>
<tr><td></td><td></td><td colspan="2">Transplanting</td><td></td><td colspan="2">Transplanting</td><td></td><td>Transplanting</td><td></td><td></td><td></td></tr>
<tr><td></td><td></td><td></td><td></td><td></td><td colspan="2">Leaf cutting</td><td></td><td></td><td></td><td></td><td></td></tr>
<tr><td></td><td></td><td></td><td colspan="6">Fertilizing</td><td></td><td></td><td></td></tr>
<tr><td></td><td></td><td></td><td></td><td colspan="3">Wire placing/ removal</td><td></td><td></td><td></td><td></td><td></td></tr>
</table>

MANAGEMENT TIPS

Placement	Place in a well-lit and well-ventilated area. Avoid late afternoon sunlight during summer. Move under cover during winter.
Watering	It's weak to draining. When the surface of the soil is dry, give plenty of water.
Fertilizing	Give solid fertilizer.
Pest Damage	Be careful of aphids, scale insects and root carcinoma.
Transplanting	Once every two years. Best time is March–April or June–July.

PREPARING A KENGAI

Before: Early March

→

After: Early March

TRANSPLANTING (EARLY MARCH)

1 Cut the longer roots using rooting scissors. If the plant was previously in a large pot, cut about half of the roots at the sides.

2 If you find any diseased roots, cut them using rooting scissors and remove.

TIP

Chojubai is very weak to root carcinoma.

3 Place the tree (up to the "neck") in a liquid solution and soak for 1–2 hours. Then remove and drain off excess water. Don't dispose of the solution yet.

TIP

For liquid treatment, fill a 2.5 gallon (10 l) bucket to 70/80% with water, then add about two caps of liquid treatment.

4 Prepare the pot and the lower soil (80% akadama medium grain; 20% river sand. Add around 10% worth of bamboo charcoal as well).

※Use a mixture of 80% akadama medium grain, 20% river sand, and add about 10% bamboo charcoal.

TIP

Don't place the bamboo charcoal on the surface of the soil; it will float if you immerse the pot in water.

5 Put the rest of the soil on the top (80% akadama small grain; 20% river sand).

※Use a mixture of 80% akadama small grain, 20% river sand.

6 Make sure there are no gaps, using tweezers or a bamboo skewer to fill in.

7 Immerse the pot in the solution for around 1–2 hours.

8 Appearance of the tree after transplanting is completed and moss has been spread.

MAKING A MOYOGI (STRIPED TREE) OUT OF A TREE THAT GREW IN A FIELD

Before: Early June

→

After: Early June

PRUNING (EARLY JUNE)

TIP

Chojubai's shoots grow easily. Cut them often.

1 Use pruning scissors to cut the shoots coming out from the lower area and make the area around the trunk less crowded.

2 Appearance after cutting the shoots.

3 Use pruning scissors to cut overgrown branches.

4 Appearance after pruning.

LEAF CUTTING (EARLY APRIL)

1 Use leaf-cutting scissors to cut leaves at their base.

2 Appearance after leaves are cut.

WIRING (EARLY JUNE)

1 Wrap one branch at a time and arrange the branches.

2 Appearance after the wiring and arranging are completed.

ARRANGING (EARLY JUNE)

1 Hold the tip of branches with tweezers and bend them tightly in a sharp angle.

2 Appearance after arranging.

TRANSPLANTING (EARLY JUNE)

1 Scoop the roots downwards with a rake.

2 Cut the long roots using rooting scissors.

3 Cut the main root with branch-cutting scissors.

4 Appearance after cutting is completed.

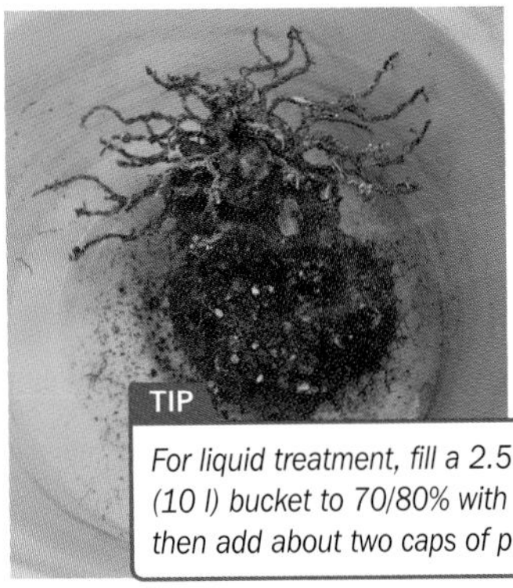

5 Place the tree in treatment solution for half an hour (immerse to the base of the trunk).

TIP

For liquid treatment, fill a 2.5 gallon (10 l) bucket to 70/80% with water, then add about two caps of product.

6 Prepare the pot and the soil (akadama medium grain; add also 10% of bamboo charcoal and mix).

※Akadama (medium grain), also add 10% of bamboo charcoal and mix well.

TIP

Don't place the bamboo charcoal on the surface of the soil; it will float if you immerse the pot in water.

7 Place the tree and apply the top layer of soil (akadama small grain).

※Akadama small grain.

8 Bend the wire around one point with pliers and fix the tree.

9 Repeat step **5**, for the potted bonsai: immerse the pot in the solution for 1–2 hours.

10 Appearance after transplanting is completed.

※Tips for good flowering = trim the tips of new branches, and use the solid type of phosphoric acid/potassium fertilizer.

Moyogi, 6 in (15 cm) height,
Rei pot

Tsubaki 椿

PROFILE

OTHER NAMES *Camillia japonica*
CLASS Theaceae, Camellia (evergreen)
TREE SHAPE Shakan, Moyogi, Kengai, Yoseue

A calm and graceful look, with plenty of flower shape and color varieties

Called the "Japanese camellia," Yabu Tsubaki grows on the Pacific side, whereas Yuki Tsubaki grows in the snowy areas by the Sea of Japan. Both species can be combined into over a thousand varieties that change in flower shape and color. Varieties with smaller flowers are better suited for bonsai. This plant has enjoyed status since ancient times, and mention of it appears in many early Japanese stories such as *Manyoshu*, *Kojiki* and *Nihongi*.

MANAGEMENT TIPS

Placement Place in a well-ventilated area. This plant likes direct/dappled sunlight in the morning and shade in the afternoon. Shelter the plant in winter, before the first frost.

Watering Needs will vary according to season, with less water being needed in winter.

Fertilizing Use solid fertilizer.

Pest Damage Be careful of moths and anthrax.

Transplanting Once every two years, between April and June.

ACTION CALENDAR

Jan	Feb	Mar	Apr	May	Jun	Jul	Aug	Sep	Oct	Nov	Dec
			Transplanting								
			Sprout plucking								
			Fertilizing					Fertilizing			
			Wire placing/ removal								

PREPARING A HALF KENGAI

Before: Early April

After: Early April

PRUNING (EARLY APRIL)

1 Prune branches that stopped growing, using pruning scissors.

TIP

If you prune branches as these ones, the buds will bloom well.

WIRING/BRANCH ARRANGING (EARLY APRIL)

1 Wrap one branch at a time and arrange them.

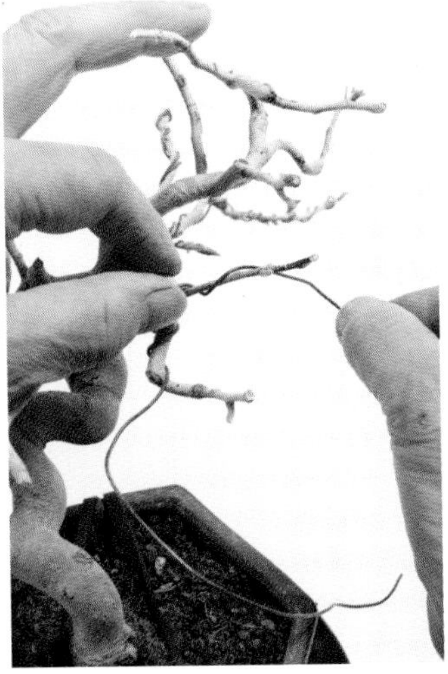

2 Appearance after wiring and branch arranging are completed.

TRANSPLANTING (EARLY APRIL)

1 Appearance after scooping the roots and cutting the longer ones using rooting scissors.

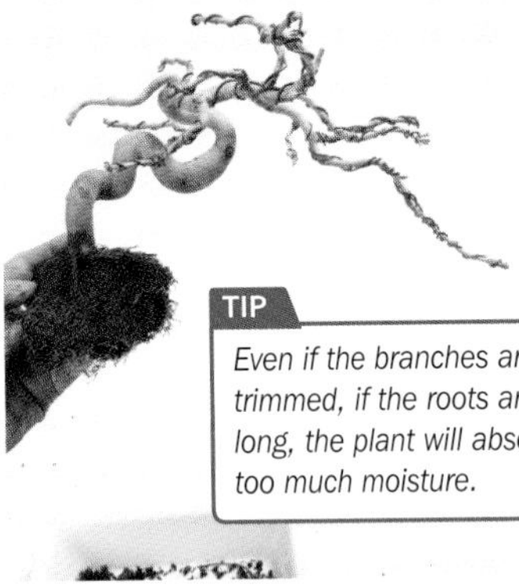

TIP

Even if the branches are well trimmed, if the roots are left long, the plant will absorb too much moisture.

2 Prepare the pot and the lower soil (akadama medium grain; add around 10% worth of kanuma soil and mix).

※Akadama (medium grain), add around 10% of kanuma soil and mix.

3 Appearance after transplanting is completed and moss has been spread.

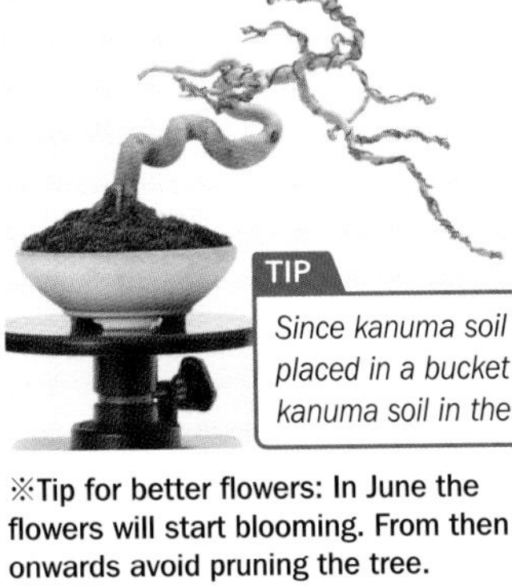

TIP

Since kanuma soil is light, it will float if placed in a bucket of water, so only mix kanuma soil in the bottom part of the soil.

※Tip for better flowers: In June the flowers will start blooming. From then onwards avoid pruning the tree.

Tosamizuki 土佐水木

PROFILE

OTHER NAMES Hyuuga mizuki, Iyomizuki
CLASS Hamamelidaceae, Corylopsis (deciduous shrub)
TREE SHAPE Shakan, BunJingi, Moyogi, Fukinagashi, Kengai and others

Soukan, 6¼ in (16 cm) height,
Fujikake Yuyama pot

Pretty eye-catching flowers in early spring exhibitions

It's native to the mountains of the Kochi prefecture. The blooming process starts with the tips of the leaves growing upwards, followed by small yellow flowers blooming all over. Despite being in the same family and also often grown as bonsai, the Hyuuga Mizuki has shorter spikes. These trees are often brought to bonsai exhibitions in early spring, where their pretty flowers catch the eyes of many. In order to maintain healthy flowers, be careful to not cut the leaves.

ACTION CALENDAR

Action	Jan	Feb	Mar	Apr	May	Jun	Jul	Aug	Sep	Oct	Nov	Dec
Transplanting			■	■								
Sprout Cutting				■	■							
Fertilizing				■	■	■			■	■		
Wire placing/ removal			■	■	■	■	■					

MANAGEMENT TIPS

Placement Place in a well-lit and well-ventilated area. In summer, avoid sunlight in late afternoon. It's very weak to frost; move it under cover in winter.

Watering When the surface dries, gives plenty of water.

Fertilizing Use solid fertilizer.

Pest Damage Be careful of powdery mildew.

Transplanting Once every two years. Best done between March and April.

CHANGING THE FAÇADE (MAIN POINT OF VIEW SIDE) OF THE TREE

Before: Early March

→

After: Early March

→

After: Mid-May

WIRING/BRANCH ARRANGING (EARLY MARCH)

1 Arrange branches to change the facade of the tree. Wrap one branch at a time and arrange them.

2 Appearance after wiring and branch arranging are completed.

TRANSPLANTING (EARLY APRIL)

1 Scoop the roots downwards with a rake.

2 Cut the longer roots using rooting scissors.

3 Appearance after cutting the roots.

4 Prepare the pot and the lower soil (akadama medium grain 80%; river sand 20%, add around 10% bamboo charcoal to the mix).

※Use a mixture of 80% akadama medium grain, 20% river sand, and add about 10% bamboo charcoal.

5 Place the soil and fix the tree by bending the wire in a cross shape.

TIP

Since this tree is tall, placing wire in a cross shape makes it easier to fix the tree.

6 Apply top layer of soil and make sure to leave no gaps in the soil (akadama small grain 80%; river sand 20%).

TIP

Don't place the bamboo charcoal on the surface of the soil; it will float if you immerse the pot in water.

※Use a mixture of 80% akadama small grain, 20% river sand.

7 Appearance after transplanting is completed and moss is spread.

SPROUT CUTTING (MID-MAY)

1 Appearance of grown sprouts.

2 Use pruning scissors to cut the sprouts.

3 Appearance after cutting is completed.

※Tip for improving flower growth: Pluck the tip of new sprouts and use fertilizer rich in phosphoric acid and potassium.

Nobara 野薔薇

Flowers bloom in early June

Moyogi, 4¼ in (11 cm) height, round pot

PROFILE

OTHER NAMES Noibara
CLASS Rosaceae (deciduous shrub)
TREE SHAPE Moyogi, Shakan, Kabutachi, Hankengai, Ishitsuki

A species popular for its wild appearance, has small flowers and red fruits

Originally a wild Rosacea, native to Japan. It is often used in cultivation for breeding with other flowers. In the case of bonsai, the most commonly grown varieties are those with small rose-like (pink or white) flowers. In the fall, it grows lovely little red fruits. Give plenty of fertilizer, also during flower blooming season.

ACTION CALENDAR

Jan	Feb	Mar	Apr	May	Jun	Jul	Aug	Sep	Oct	Nov	Dec
	Transplanting	Transplanting						Transplanting	Transplanting		
			Fertilizing	Fertilizing	Fertilizing				■		
				Wire placing/ removal	Wire placing/ removal						

MANAGEMENT TIPS

Placement Place in a well-lit and well-ventilated area. It can also grow in partial shade. During winter move under cover.

Watering When the surface of the soil is dry, give plenty of water. Be careful not to let it dry out during summer.

Fertilizing Use solid fertilizer.

Pest Damage Be careful of aphids, scale insects, black spots, powdery mildew and root carcinoma.

Transplanting Once every two years. Best time is between February and March or between September and October.

TRANSPLANTING TO A BONSAI POT

Before: Mid-May

→

After: Mid-May

PRUNING (MID-MAY)

1 Prune the branches that are too crowded with branch-cutting scissors.

2 Appearance after pruning.

WIRING/BRANCH ARRANGING (MID-MAY)

1 Wrap one branch at a time and arrange them.

2 Appearance after wiring and branch arranging are completed.

TRANSPLANTING (MID-MAY)

※After the first transplanting, timing will change to between February and March.

1 Remove the plastic pot.

2 Cut the sides of the roots using rooting scissors.

3 Cut the longer roots on the sides.

4 Appearance after cutting is completed.

5 Prepare the pot and the lower soil (akadama medium grain 80%; river sand 20%).

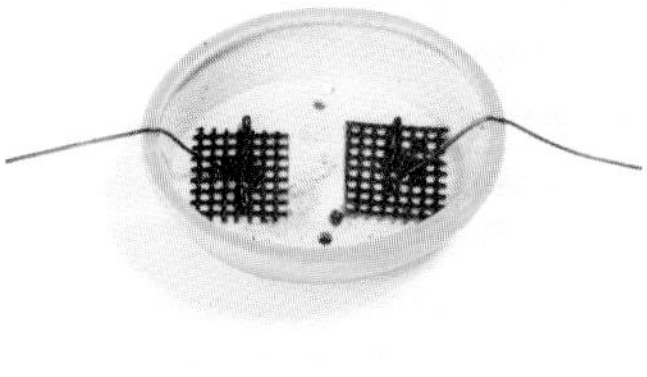

※Use a mixture of 80% akadama small grain, 20% river sand.

6 Place the tree, apply top layer of soil (akadama small grain 80%; river sand 20%).

※Soil used on top: akadama (small grain) 80%, river sand 20%.

7 Use tweezers to make sure to leave no gaps in the soil.

8 Appearance after transplanting is completed and moss is spread.

※Tip for improving flower growth: Pluck the tip of new sprouts, use fertilizer rich in phosphoric acid and potassium.

Shakan, 6¼ in (16 cm) height,
10¾ in (27 cm) width, Japanese style pot

Boke 木瓜

PROFILE

OTHER NAMES Karaboke
CLASS Rosaceae, Chaenomeles (deciduous shrub)
TREE SHAPE Soukan, Shakan, Kengai, Kabutachi, Moyogi

Whether early blooming or late blooming, its crimson flowers are popular

Also known as "Japanese quince," it has an early-blooming variety (Kamboke) and a late-blooming one (Haruboke). The tree shape is easy to arrange and change. Flowers may be pink, white, red or reddish orange in color, and may be single or double. In the fall, the tree bears little fruits.

ACTION CALENDAR

Jan	Feb	Mar	Apr	May	Jun	Jul	Aug	Sep	Oct	Nov	Dec
	Tree Cutting			Leaf cutting				Transplanting			
			Fertilizing					Fertilizing			
Wire placing/ removal											

MANAGEMENT TIPS

Placement Place in a well-lit and well-ventilated area. Keep outdoors until flowers blossom.

Watering It gets dry easily. Be careful to not let it dry out during spring and summer.

Fertilizing Give solid fertilizer.

Pest Damage Be careful of aphids, scale insects and root carcinoma.

Transplanting Once every two years. It's best done between September and October. *If done in spring, it'll most likely cause root carcinoma, so absolutely do not transplant in spring.

MAKING A FUKINAGASHI (WINDSOCK)

Before: Mid-May

→

After: Mid-May

WIRING (MID-MAY)

1 Appearance of grown new sprouts.

2 Wrap each new sprout with wire and arrange them.

3 Appearance after wiring and arranging.

LEAF CUTTING (MID-MAY)

1 Appearance of grown leaves.

2 Cut leaves at their base with leaf-cutting scissors.

3 Appearance after leaf cutting is completed.

※Tips for good flowering: Trim the tips of new branches, and use the solid type of phosphoric acid/potassium-rich fertilizer.

Yukiyanagi 雪柳

Red flowers

Shakan, 7 in (18 cm) height, Tsuchi pot

White flowers

PROFILE

OTHER NAMES Spirae, *Spiraea thunbergii*
CLASS Rosaceae, Spiraea (deciduous shrub)
TREE SHAPE Shakan, Moyogi, Yoseue

Willowy, thin branches with small snowdrop-like flowers

Native to Japan and China. Despite being called a Yanagi (willow), in reality this is a species of Rosacea. In very early spring, it grows small white flowers that look like snow. Thin branches that look like they are shivering in the wind add even more grace and elegance. There are white and red flower varieties.

ACTION CALENDAR

Jan	Feb	Mar	Apr	May	Jun	Jul	Aug	Sep	Oct	Nov	Dec
		Transplanting	Transplanting		Tree Cutting	Tree Cutting		Transplanting			
			Fertilizing	Fertilizing				Fertilizing	Fertilizing		
		Wire placing/ removal	Wire placing/ removal				Wire placing/ removal	Wire placing/ removal			

MANAGEMENT TIPS

Placement Place in a well-lit and well-ventilated area. Avoid late afternoon sunlight during summer. Move under cover during winter.

Watering It likes water. Be careful to not let it dry out during summer.

Fertilizing Give solid fertilizer.

Pest Damage Be careful of aphids.

Transplanting Once every two years. Transplant between March and April or in September.

MAKING A SOUKAN

Before: Early April

→

After: Early April

→

After: Mid-June

PRUNING (EARLY APRIL)

1 Prune the longer branches using pruning scissors.

2 Appearance after pruning.

WIRING/BRANCH ARRANGING (LATE APRIL)

1 Wrap one branch at a time and arrange them.

2 Appearance after wiring and branch arranging are completed.

TRANSPLANTING (EARLY APRIL)

1 Scoop the roots with a rake downwards, then cut the longer roots using rooting scissors.

2 Appearance after cutting the roots.

3 Prepare the pot and the lower soil (akadama medium grain 80%, river sand 20%).

※Use a mixture of 80% akadama medium grain, 20% river sand.

4 Place the tree and insert the wire from the bottom. Bend the wire with pliers in a U shape and arrange it downwards. Cut the excess wire and repeat the process on the other side.

TIP

This method is ideal when the pot is small and has only one hole in the bottom.

5 Appearance after transplanting is completed and moss is spread.

PRUNING (EARLY APRIL)

1 Appearance of grown sprouts.

2 Prune the longer branches using pruning scissors.

3 Appearance after pruning.

※Tip for improving flower growth: Pluck the tip of new sprouts, use fertilizer rich in phosphoric acid and potassium.

Negari, 7 in (18 cm) height, Shuzan pot

Rengyou 連翹

PROFILE

OTHER NAMES Weeping forsythia
CLASS Oleaceae, Forsythia (deciduous shrub)
TREE SHAPE Negari, Kengai, Kabutachi, Moyogi, Shakan

It draws attention with its early blooming flowers, and is a charming tree to grow

Native to China, this tree was imported in the Heian period. After the point at which branches rise, many flowers bloom at once. Roots are very strong, and they resist even strong cuts and the creating of Neagari. As it's so resilient, it's easy to arrange into various shapes. The roots spread quickly, so transplanting is done twice a year. Pictured here is a large-flowered variety.

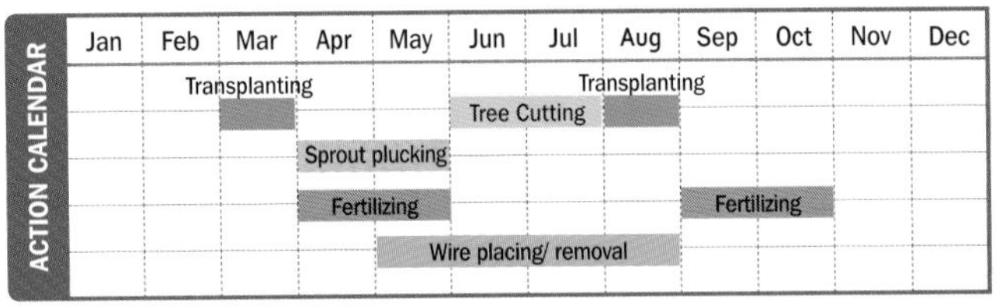

MANAGEMENT TIPS

Placement Place in a well-lit and well-ventilated area. If left in shade, the flowers will be ruined.

Watering It likes water. Don't let it dry out during flower blooming season.

Fertilizing Give solid fertilizer.

Pest Damage Be careful of scale insects and spider mites.

Transplanting Twice per year, either in March or August.

MAKING A NEAGARI (RISING ROOTS)

Before: Early March

→

After: Early March

→

After: Mid-March

TRANSPLANTING (EARLY MARCH)

TIP

Rengyou has an impressive root growth rate.

1 Appearance of grown and bent roots.

2 Scoop the roots downwards using a rake.

3 Appearance after scooping the roots.

4 Wrap and fix tightly the base of the roots with metal wire.

5 Wrap the roots in a downward spiral.

6 Appearance of roots after being wrapped in wire.

7 Cut the longer roots using rooting scissors.

8 Appearance of roots after being cut.

9 Prepare the pot and the lower soil (akadama medium grain 80%; river sand 20%. Add around 10% worth of bamboo charcoal into the mix as well).

※Use a mixture of 80% akadama medium grain, 20% river sand, and add about 10% bamboo charcoal.

10 Place soil and set the tree on top (submerge only a small part of the roots in soil).

TIP

Don't place the bamboo charcoal on the surface of the soil; it will float if you immerse the pot in water.

11 Add the top layer of soil (80% akadama small grain; 20% river sand).

※Use a mixture of 80% akadama small grain, 20% river sand.

12 Use tweezers to make sure there are no gaps in the soil and that it's evenly spread.

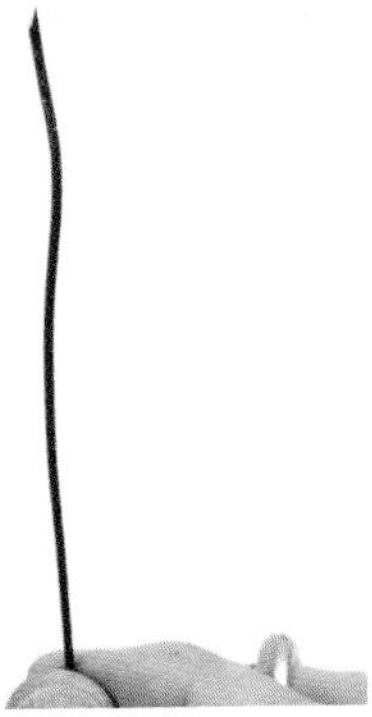

13 Sharpen the tip of a metal wire.

14 Insert the sharpened wire from the bottom of the pot.

15 Pull the sharpened wire out through the surface.

16 Bend the wire in a U shape with pliers.

17 Pull the bent wire back from the bottom.

18 Bend the wire coming out from the bottom so that it's parallel to the pot's base.

19 Cut the excess wire.

20 Repeat steps 14 to 19 on the opposite side.

21 Appearance after fixing both sides of the tree and water moss has been spread.

WIRING/BRANCH ARRANGING (MID-MAY)

1 Appearance of new sprouts.

2 Wrap one sprout at a time and arrange them.

3 Appearance after wiring and branch arranging are completed.

※Tip for improving flower growth: Pluck the tip of new sprouts and avoid cutting leaves.

Aotsuzurafuji 青葛藤

Kengai, 13 in (33 cm) height, 13¾ in (35 cm) width, Aokouchi round pot

PROFILE

OTHER NAMES Kamiebi, *Cocculus trilobus*
CLASS Menispermaceae
TREE SHAPE Shakan, Kengai

Grape-like fruits and a trunk overflowing with rustic beauty

This grows on mountains everywhere in Japan. Blooming starts around June with small, pale yellow flowers; later, in the fall, it grows grape-like fruits. As the tree ages, the trunk also becomes rough, and attains a rustic overall shape. Since its vines do not grow any thicker, we bring the roots up a bit at every transplant.

ACTIVITY CALENDAR

Jan	Feb	Mar	Apr	May	Jun	Jul	Aug	Sep	Oct	Nov	Dec
		Transplanting			Tree Cutting			Transplanting			
				Sprout plucking							
			Fertilizing					Fertilizing			
		Wire placing/ removal									

MANAGEMENT TIPS

Placement Place in a well-lit and well-ventilated area.

Watering When the surface of the soil is dry, give plenty of water.

Fertilizing Give solid fertilizer.

Pest Damage Be careful of aphids.

Transplanting Once every two years. Transplant between March and April or September and October.

MAKING A NEAGARI

Before: Mid-April

After: Mid-April

PRUNING (EARLY APRIL)

1 Prune withered branches using pruning scissors.

2 Cut the remains of the previous year's fruits.

TIP

By cutting the remains, we improve the quality of the next flowers.

WIRING/BRANCH ARRANGING (MID-APRIL)

1 Wrap one branch at a time and arrange them.

2 Appearance after wiring and branch arranging are completed.

TRANSPLANTING (MID-APRIL)

1 Scoop the roots downwards with a rake.

2 Cut the longer roots using rooting scissors.

3 Scoop the roots some more to remove the soil.

4 Appearance after scooping the roots.

5 Wrap tightly the base of the roots with metal wire.

6 Wrap the wire in a downwards spiral, bend the end of the wrap and cut the excess wire.

7 Appearance after wrapping the roots with wire.

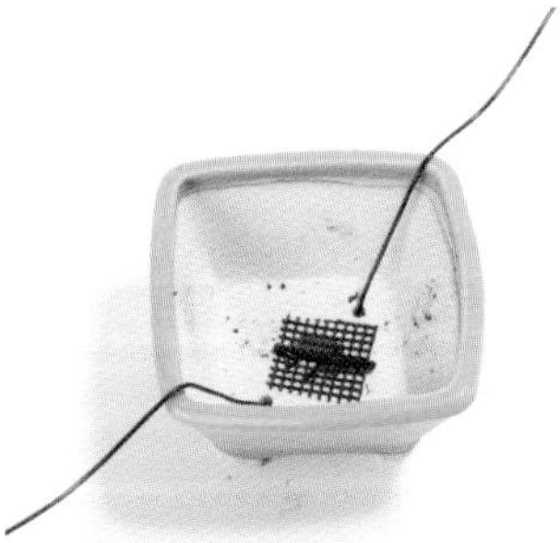

8 Prepare the pot and the soil (akadama medium 80%; river sand 20%).

※Use a mixture of 80% akadama medium grain, 20% river sand.

9 Place the tree and add the top layer of soil (akadama small 80%; river sand 20%).

※Use a mixture of 80% akadama small grain, 20% river sand.

10 Use tweezers to make sure there are no gaps in the soil.

11 Appearance after transplanting is completed and moss has been spread.

MEMO

Tips for better fruiting

The flowers will bloom in mid-June. This tree is a hermaphrodite. In May, give plenty of fertilizer.

① Place male flowers beside female flowers to facilitate natural mating.

② Place male flowers above female flowers.

Male flowers (on the right): Round pistils
Female flowers (on the left): Many flowers and plentiful pollen.

Kengai, 8½ in (22 cm) height, rainbow fountain pot

Akebi 木通

PROFILE

OTHER NAMES *Akebia quinata* "Shirobana" (5-leaf), *Akebia quinata* "Purple Rose" (3-leaf)
CLASS Lardizabalaceae
TREE SHAPE Shakan, Kengai

Unique purple fruits inspire nostalgia for mountains and fields

Native to Japanese mountains and fields. Around April, it grows little bright purple flowers. There is a three-leaf variety and a five-leaf variety, and growing the two in close proximity can result in pollination. In fall, purple fruits with white pulp will grow. Since its vines do not grow any thicker, we bring the roots up a bit at every transplant.

ACTION CALENDAR

	Jan	Feb	Mar	Apr	May	Jun	Jul	Aug	Sep	Oct	Nov	Dec
Transplanting			■						■			
Tree cutting						■	■					
Fertilizing				■	■				■	■		
Wire placing/ removal				■	■	■	■					

MANAGEMENT TIPS

Placement Place in a well-lit and well-ventilated area.

Watering When the surface of the soil is dry, give plenty of water.

Fertilizing Give solid fertilizer.

Pest Damage Be careful of powdery mildew and aphids.

Transplanting Once every two years. Best done in March or September.

MEMO

Tips for better fruiting

Grasp the male flower with tweezers →

Place it on the tip of the female flower.

When breeding flowers in April, mix as follows:

- Goyou Akebi (male) x Mitsuba Akebi (female)
- Mitsuba Akebi (male) x Goyou Akebi (female)

Mitsuba Akebi

Female Male

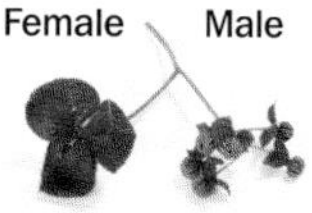

Goyou Akebi

Female Male

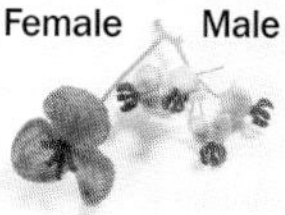

Inubiwa 犬琵琶

Kabutachi, 8 in (20 cm) height, Chinese style pot

PROFILE

OTHER NAMES Itabi, Chichinomi, Koichijiku
CLASS Moraceae
TREE SHAPE Kabutachi, Shakan, Fukinagashi

Charming, dark purple fruits and serene branches

A species of Ficus also known as the "Japanese fig," this tree naturally grows in warm areas west of the Kanto region, Honshu, Shikoku and Kyushu. There is a narrow-leaf variety and a round-leaf variety. The narrow-leaf tree is easier to arrange into desired shapes, and so tends to be the more popular choice for bonsai. In early summer, it grows fruit-like produce near leaves; however, these are flowers and not fruits. In fall, they will turn a dark violet color similar to blueberries.

ACTION CALENDAR	Jan	Feb	Mar	Apr	May	Jun	Jul	Aug	Sep	Oct	Nov	Dec
Transplanting			Transplanting						Transplanting			
Tree cutting						Tree cutting	Tree cutting					
Sprout Cutting					Sprout Cutting	Sprout Cutting						
Fertilizing				Fertilizing	Fertilizing				Fertilizing	Fertilizing		
Wire placing/ removal			Wire placing/ removal	Wire placing/ removal	Wire placing/ removal	Wire placing/ removal	Wire placing/ removal	Wire placing/ removal				

MANAGEMENT TIPS

Placement Place in a well-lit and well-ventilated area.

Watering When the surface of the soil is dry, give plenty of water.

Fertilizing Give solid fertilizer.

Pest Damage Be careful of scale insects and black fly.

Transplanting Once every two years. Best done in March or September.

MAKING A KABUTACHI

Before: Early March

→

After: Early March

WIRING (EARLY MARCH)

1 Wrap one branch at a time and bend them to one side making them look blown by the wind.

TIP

Doing this will stop sap from emerging.

2 If there's any scarring on the trunk, apply healing coating agent with a hard brush/spatula.

TRANSPLANTING (EARLY MARCH)

1 Cut the sides of the roots using rooting scissors.

2 Cut the main root using branch-cutting scissors.

3 Appearance after cutting the roots.

※From now on the details of the activity are on p. 37. Use akadama medium grain 80%; river sand 20%.

4 Appearance after transplanting is completed and moss has been spread.

SPROUT CUTTING (MID-MAY)

1 Cut the overgrown sprouts using pruning scissors

MEMO

Tip for better fruiting

This tree is a hermaphrodite. The growths that seem like fruits (shown in photo) are actually flowers. Their breeding is unique, as inside the flower sac the parasitic chalcid wasps grow and they act as intermediaries for the pollen. In mid-May small fruits begin; these turn dark violet in the fall.

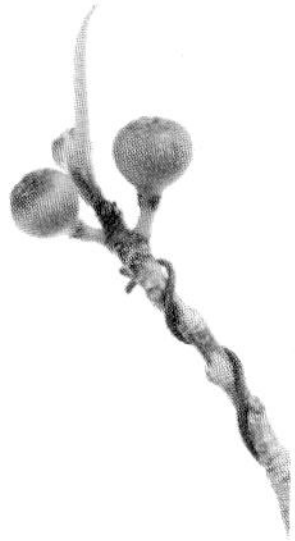

Moyogi, 3¼ in (8 cm) height, Imari pot

Umemodoki 梅擬

PROFILE

OTHER NAMES Japanese winterberry
CLASS Aquifoliaceae
TREE SHAPE Soukan, Shakan, Moyogi, Kabutachi, Yoseue

Pretty small red fruits, but protect them from birds!

Lasting from the fall into winter, the small, bright red fruits can be appreciated for a long time. White and yellow fruits can also occasionally be seen growing on this tree. In order to improve fruiting, place male flowers near female flowers. Birds like the taste of Umemodoki fruits, so be sure to protect your tree by placing a net basket over it.

ACTION CALENDAR	Jan	Feb	Mar	Apr	May	Jun	Jul	Aug	Sep	Oct	Nov	Dec
Transplanting												
Sprout plucking												
Fertilizing												
Wire placing/ removal												

MANAGEMENT TIPS

Placement Place in a well-lit and well-ventilated area. Do not expose new sprouts to cold. In summer, move it to shade during the afternoon. In winter, move under cover.

Watering If left without water, the fruits will be ruined. When fruits emerge, give plenty of water.

Fertilizing Give solid fertilizer.

Pest Damage Be careful of aphids, scale insects and black spots.

Transplanting Once every year. Best done in March or early April

MAKING A SHAKAN

Before: Early April

→

After: Early April

→

After: Mid-May

PRUNING (EARLY APRIL)

1 Cut branches that ruin the shape of the bonsai using pruning scissors.

2 If there are branches left uncut, cut them using pruning scissors.

3 Treat cut wounds by applying a healing coating agent with a hard brush/spatula.

TRANSPLANTING (EARLY APRIL)

1 Scoop the roots downwards with a rake.

2 Appearance after we cut the longer roots using rooting scissors.

3 Prepare the pot and the soil (akadama medium 80%; river sand 20%).

※Use a mixture of 80% akadama medium grain, 20% river sand.

4 Place the tree, and insert wire from the bottom of the pot and bend it with pliers to fix the tree. Repeat on the other side.

※More detailed explanation on page 37

5 Appearance after transplanting is completed and moss has been spread.

※Tips for better fruits through breeding: This is a hermaphrodite tree. ① If male and female flowers are placed near each other, they'll breed naturally. ② Place the female flowers on top of male flowers. ③ Grasp the male flower with tweezers, then place it on the tip of the female flower for artificial pollination.

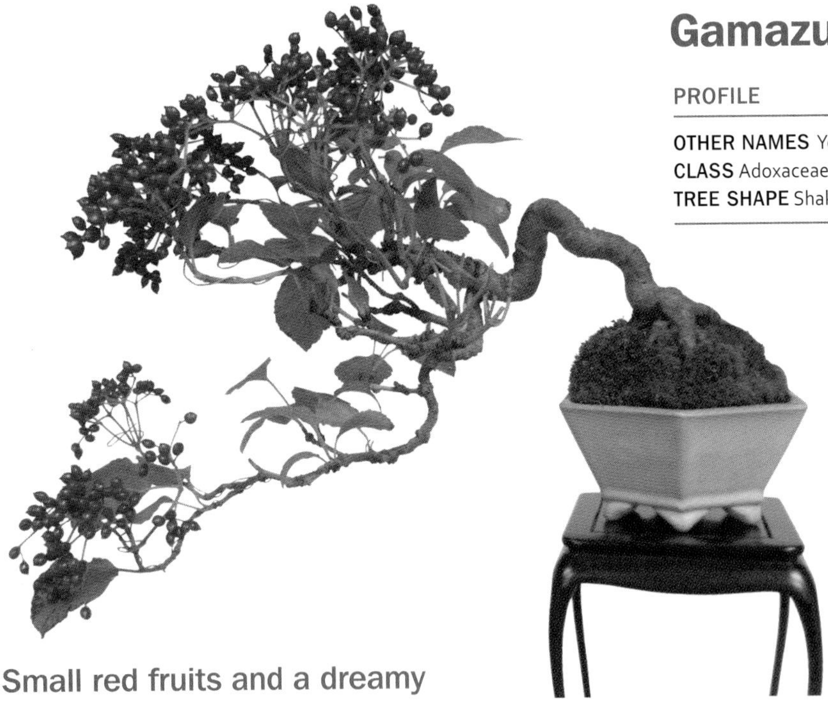

Gamazumi 荚蒾

PROFILE

OTHER NAMES Yotsudome
CLASS Adoxaceae
TREE SHAPE Shakan, Moyogi, Kengai

Hankengai, 8 in (20 cm), Bikou pot

Small red fruits and a dreamy atmosphere

Native to Japanese mountains and hills. Small white flowers bloom in May. In fall, the red fruits can be appreciated instead. A variety called "Kimino Gamazumi" is also popular for its yellow fruits. If, during pollination, it grows with other tree species, the fruiting will improve. As the tree ages, the branches become stiffer and more difficult to arrange, so wire and arrange the branches while young.

<table>
<tr><th>ACTION CALENDAR</th><th>Jan</th><th>Feb</th><th>Mar</th><th>Apr</th><th>May</th><th>Jun</th><th>Jul</th><th>Aug</th><th>Sep</th><th>Oct</th><th>Nov</th><th>Dec</th></tr>
<tr><td></td><td></td><td></td><td colspan="2">Transplanting</td><td></td><td colspan="2">Tree Cutting</td><td></td><td></td><td></td><td></td><td></td></tr>
<tr><td></td><td></td><td></td><td></td><td colspan="6">Sprout plucking</td><td></td><td></td><td></td></tr>
<tr><td></td><td></td><td></td><td></td><td colspan="2">Fertilizing</td><td></td><td></td><td></td><td colspan="2">Fertilizing</td><td></td><td></td></tr>
<tr><td></td><td></td><td></td><td></td><td colspan="5">Wire placing/ removal</td><td></td><td></td><td></td><td></td></tr>
</table>

MANAGEMENT TIPS

Placement Place in a well-lit and well-ventilated area.

Watering When the surface of the soil is dry, give plenty of water. In summer, water twice daily.

Fertilizing Give solid fertilizer.

Pest Damage Be careful of brown spots, powdery mildew, scale insects and *Pyrrhalta humeralis*.

Transplanting Once every year. Best done between March and April or in September.

TRANSPLANTING TO A POT THAT MATCHES THE SHAPE OF THE TREE

Before: Early April

Before: Early November

After: Mid-May

After: Early April

WIRING/BRANCH ARRANGING (EARLY APRIL)

1 Wrap one branch at a time and arrange them.

2 Appearance after wiring and branch arranging are completed.

TRANSPLANTING (EARLY APRIL)

1 Cut the sides of the roots using rooting scissors.

2 Cut the roots vertically using rooting scissors.

3 Use a rake to scoop the roots downwards.

4 Appearance of cut roots.

5 Prepare the pot and the soil (akadama medium 80%; river sand 20%).

※Use a mixture of 80% akadama medium grain, 20% river sand.

6 Appearance after transplanting is completed and moss has been spread.

※Tips to improve fruiting: When the flowers open, we put pollen from other Gamazumi on them.

Kamatsuma 鎌柄

PROFILE

OTHER NAMES Ushikoroshi
CLASS Rosaceae
TREE SHAPE Shakan, Moyogi, Kabutachi, Kengai, Yoseue

Hankengai, 7 in (18 cm) height

Lots of branches with red fruits, plus red and yellow leaves in the fall

It grows in Japanese mountain and hill areas. Around May it grows white flowers. In fall, it grows red fruits. It's been called "sickle grip" (kamatsuma) in Japan because its hard wood has been used for making the handles of tools. Its other nickname, "cow killer" (ushikoroshi), comes from the density of its branches. A cow whose horns are caught in the branches would be a trapped animal indeed.

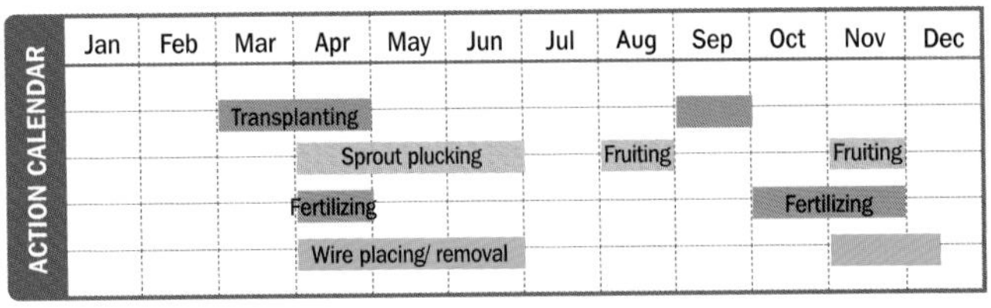

MANAGEMENT TIPS

Placement From blooming to fruiting, place under direct sunlight. In summer, avoid direct sunlight in the afternoon. In winter move under cover.

Watering Be careful to not let it dry out.

Fertilizing Give solid fertilizer.

Pest Damage Be careful of moths.

Transplanting Once every year. Best done between March and April or September.

TRANSPLANTING TO A POT WITH BETTER BALANCE

Before: Early April

→

Before: Early November

→

After: Early April

→

After: Mid-May

PRUNING (EARLY APRIL)

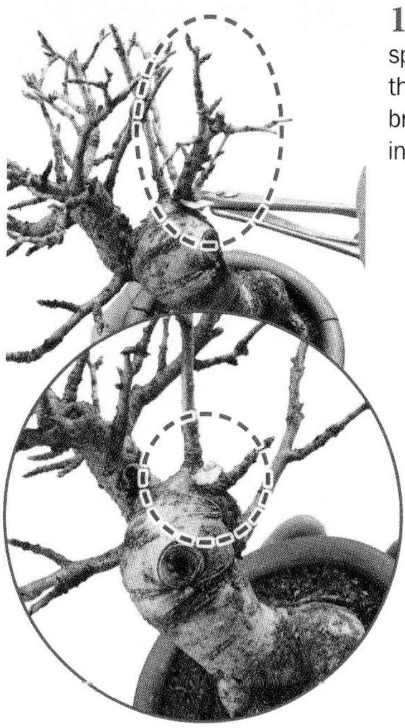

1 Cut branches that spoil the shape of the bonsai (standing branches) using pruning scissors.

2 Cut branches that spoil the shape of the bonsai (such as long protruding branches) using pruning scissors.

3 Apply healing coating agent with a hard brush/spatula on the cut wounds.

WIRING/BRANCH ARRANGING (EARLY APRIL)

1 Wrap one branch at a time and arrange them.

2 Appearance after wiring and branch arranging are completed.

TRANSPLANTING (EARLY APRIL)

1 Cut vertically into the roots. Rooting scissors are best, although pruning scissors were used here.

2 Use a rake to scoop the roots downwards and cut the longer roots using rooting scissors.

3 Appearance after cutting the roots.

4 Prepare the pot and the soil (akadama medium 80%; river sand 20%).

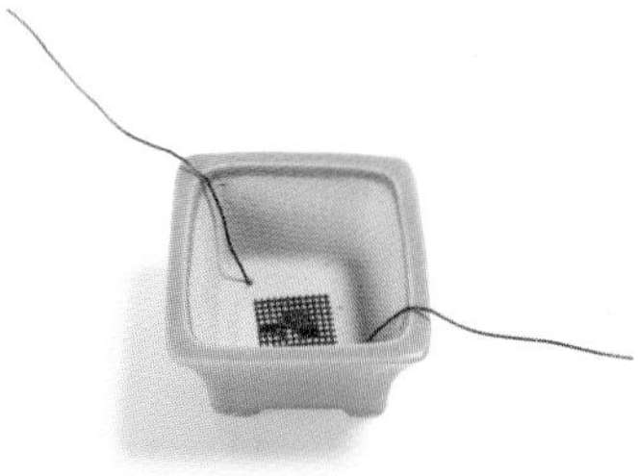

※Use a mixture of 80% akadama medium grain, 20% river sand.

5 Place the tree and the top layer of soil (akadama small 80%; river sand 20%).

※Use a mixture of 80% akadama small grain, 20% river sand.

6 Appearance after transplanting is completed and moss has been spread.

※Tip to improve fruit quality: As long as you avoid watering the flowers, fruits will grow healthily without requiring additional help.

Moyogi, 6¾ in (17 cm) height, Gekkou pot

Karin 花梨

PROFILE

OTHER NAMES Chinese quince
CLASS Rosaceae
TREE SHAPE Chokkan, Shakan, Moyogi, Kabutachi, Kengai

Charming, majestic branches and a glorious golden fruit

This was imported from China in the Heian period. It's often praised as the "King of Mimono Bonsai" due to its thick branches and majestic appearance. Its value depends on the position of the fruit. The flowers are pink and beautiful, the trunk has a striped pattern and the yellow leaves are gorgeous.

ACTIVITY CALENDAR

Jan	Feb	Mar	Apr	May	Jun	Jul	Aug	Sep	Oct	Nov	Dec
	Transplanting							Transplanting			
			Sprout Cutting	Sprout Cutting	Sprout Cutting						
			Fertilizing	Fertilizing	Fertilizing			Fertilizing	Fertilizing		
			Wire placing/removal	Wire placing/removal	Wire placing/removal						

TIP

Be careful of Gymnosporangium!

When the temperature gets above 68°F/°20°C, the bacteria *Gymnosporangium* is airborne. Since it usually spreads in April, spray fungicide disinfectant in mid–early April to protect the tree.

MANAGEMENT TIPS

Placement Place in a well-lit and well-ventilated area. In summer, cover tightly with a cheesecloth. It resists cold.

Watering It likes water. Be careful not to let it dry out during summer.

Fertilizing Give solid fertilizer.

Pest Damage Be careful of *Gymnosporangium*. Sprinkle with fungicide in spring to avoid it.

Transplanting Once every year. Best done in February or September.

TRANSPLANTING TO A BONSAI POT

Before: Mid-February

→

After: Mid-February

→

After: Mid-June

TRANSPLANTING (MID-FEBRUARY)

1 Use a rake to scoop the roots downwards.

2 Appearance of roots after scooping them.

3 Cut the longer roots using rooting scissors.

4 Appearance of roots after the longer roots have been cut.

5 Prepare the pot and the lower soil (akadama medium grain with 10% of bamboo charcoal added and mixed in).

※Use a mixture of 80% akadama medium grain, 20% river sand, and add about 10% bamboo charcoal.

6 Add the lower soil and fix the tree.

7 If the roots seem loose, put wire in a circle around the base of the trunk.

8 Twist the wire.

9 Cut the excess in wire with pliers.

10 Place the wire and push it down in the soil.

TIP

By doing this we can hold down loose roots.

11 Insert wire through the bottom of the pot and bend it in a U shape with pliers.

12 Pull the wire back down from the bottom and fold back the excess at the base.

13 Tighten the wire to fix the tree and cut the excess wire with pliers.

TIP

Don't place the bamboo charcoal on the surface of the soil; it will float if you immerse the pot in water.

14 Add the top layer of soil and use tweezers to make sure there are no gaps in the soil (akadama small grain 80%; river sand 20%).

SPREADING WATER MOSS (MID-FEBRUARY)

1 Soak water moss in water and shape it into a string.

2 Place water moss with tweezers on the soil and push it gently with your fingertips to fix it.

3 Bend thin metal wire in a U shape.

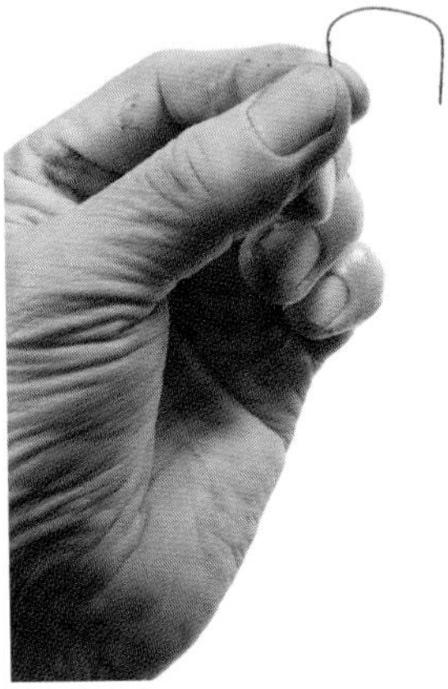

4 Place the U-shaped wires around the circumference of the pot.

※For clarity, the wire shown here is a bit thicker than is normally used.

5 Appearance after transplanting and water moss has been spread.

MEMO

Is it okay if the bark starts to peel?

Sometimes the bark peels naturally. Don't be concerned, as this is a part of the tree's growth process.

SPROUT CUTTING (MID-JUNE)

TIP

For sprout cutting, we start in April and we repeat the process multiple times.

1 Appearance of grown sprouts.

2 Cut the overgrown sprouts using pruning scissors.

3 Appearance after sprout cutting.

MEMO

Tip for better fruiting

Fruits start growing in late April and May. Being a hermaphrodite tree, it will most likely self-breed. However, fruit growth can be improved by artificial pollination. To do this, place the male flowers by a female flowers.

Kangumi 寒茱萸

Moyogi, 7½ in (19 cm) height, incense leaf pot.

PROFILE

OTHER NAMES Nawashirogumi, Marubagumi, Tawaragumi, Tokiwagumi
CLASS Elaeagnaceae
TREE SHAPE Shakan, Moyogi, Kabutachi, Hankengai

With scarlet fruits hanging from its branches, it is a wonderful evergreen in winter

Over fifteen varieties are native to Japan. Among them, the most suitable for bonsai is Nawashiro Gumi. Flowers are white or pale yellow, and the tree will always produce fruits if the flowers bloom. Around November, the hanging fruits will turn their typical scarlet color and can be enjoyed until March.

ACTION CALENDAR

Jan	Feb	Mar	Apr	May	Jun	Jul	Aug	Sep	Oct	Nov	Dec
		Transplanting									
	Leaf cutting:				Leaf cutting:						
			Sprout plucking		Sprout Cutting						
				Fertilizing				Fertilizing			
	Wire placing								Wire removal		

MANAGEMENT TIPS

Placement Place in a well-lit and well-ventilated area. In summer, avoid direct sunlight, in winter move under cover.

Watering It likes water. When the surface of the soil is dry, give plenty of water.

Fertilizing Give solid fertilizer. Do not give fertilizer in the period between blooming and fruit growth.

Pest Damage Be careful of aphids, spider mites and scale insects. As a countermeasure against birds, when fruits are growing, cover with net to protect it.

Transplanting Once per year. Best done between March and April or in September.

TRANSPLANTING INTO A SHALLOW POT

Before: Early March

→

After: Early March

LEAF CUTTING (EARLY MARCH)

1 Cut leaves at their base with leaf-cutting scissors

TIP

In the case of evergreens, we cut their leaves. Doing so will encourage more sprouts to appear.

2 Appearance after leaf cutting.

WIRING/BRANCH ARRANGING (EARLY APRIL)

1 Wrap one branch at a time and arrange them.

2 Appearance after wiring and branch arranging are completed.

TRANSPLANTING (EARLY MARCH)

1 Use a rake to scoop the roots downwards.

2 Cut the longer roots using rooting scissors.

3 Appearance of roots after the longer roots are cut.

4 Prepare the pot and the lower soil (akadama medium grain with 10% of bamboo charcoal added and mixed in).

※Use a mixture of 80% akadama medium grain, 20% river sand, and add about 10% bamboo charcoal.

TIP

Since this tree is tall, placing wire in a cross shape makes it easier to fix the tree.

5 Place the soil and fix the tree by bending the wire in a cross shape.

TIP

Don't place the bamboo charcoal on the surface of the soil; it will float if you immerse the pot in water.

※Use a mixture of 80% akadama small grain, 20% river sand.

6 Apply top layer of soil (akadama small grain 80%; river sand 20%).

7 Use tweezers to make sure there are no gaps in between the soil.

8 Appearance after transplanting is completed and moss is spread.

SPROUT CUTTING (MID-MAY)

1 Appearance of grown sprouts.

2 Cut overgrown sprouts using pruning scissors

3 Appearance after sprout cutting is completed.

MEMO

Tips for better fruits

Placing various types of Kangumi side-by-side will raise the quality of the fruits. Kangumi doesn't distinguish between male and female flowers.

Neagari, 6 in (15 cm) height,
Japanese styled Hexagon pot

Kinzu 金豆

PROFILE

OTHER NAMES Mamekinkan
CLASS Rutaceae
TREE SHAPE Moyogi, Kengai

With seed-like yellow fruits, it gives a sense of warmth

Originally from China and related to the small Mandarin orange (Kinkan), it was called "Golden citrus fruit" (Kin no yuzu). It's typically from warm areas, so it's strong to heat but weak to cold. It will bloom and surely grow fruit if it's grown in 86°F/30°C or more for a prolonged period. The round orange fruits last a long time.

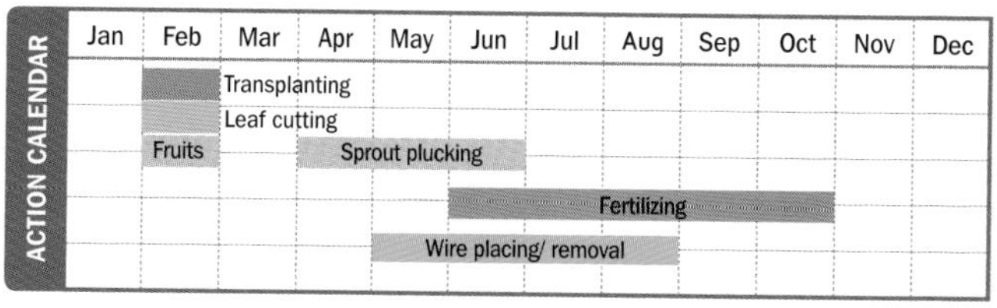

MANAGEMENT TIPS

Placement Keep under sunlight between spring and fall. Keep indoors during December. For the rest of the year, place in a well-lit and well-ventilated area.

Watering It likes water. Don't let it dry out during summer.

Fertilizing Give solid fertilizer.

Pest Damage Be careful of beetles and soot.

Transplanting Once every two years. Best done in May.

GROWING A NEAGARI-LIKE BONSAI

Before: Early May

→

After: Early May

LEAF CUTTING (EARLY MAY)

1 Cut the base of the leaves using pruning scissors.

2 Appearance after leaf cutting is completed.

PRUNING (EARLY MAY)

1 Use pruning scissors to cut the "sacrifice branch" that ruins the outline of the tree shape.

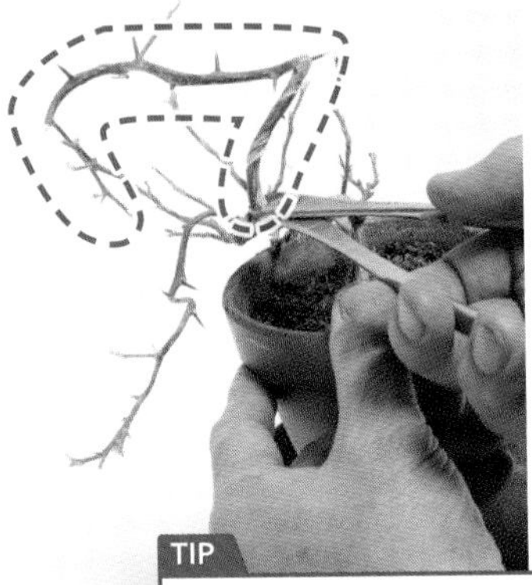

TIP

The "sacrifice branch" is a branch that we let grow longer than usual to enrich the beauty of the tree.

2 Appearance after we cut the "sacrifice branch."

3 Apply an healing coating agent on the wound with a spatula/ hard brush.

WIRING/BRANCH ARRANGING (EARLY MAY)

1 Wrap one branch at a time and arrange them.

2 Appearance after wiring and branch arrangement are completed.

TRANSPLANTING (EARLY MAY)

1 Scoop the roots downwards with a rake.

2 Wrap the roots with metal wire in a downward spiral, bend the end of the spiral with pliers and cut the excess wire.

3 Prepare the pot and the lower soil (akadama medium grain 80%; river sand 20%.)

※Use a mixture of 80% akadama medium grain, 20% river sand.

4 Place the tree and add the top layer of soil (80% akadama small grain; 20% river sand)

※Use a mixture of 80% akadama small grain, 20% river sand.

5 Appearance after transplanting is completed and moss has been spread.

※Tip for better fruiting: It's a hermaphrodite species. If flowers bloom, it will always certainly grow fruits. In summer, place it in a well-lit spot, possibly in a temperature higher than 86°F/30°C and give plenty of fertilizer.

Komayumi 小真弓

PROFILE

OTHER NAMES Spindle tree
CLASS Celastraceae
TREE SHAPE Shakan, Soukan, Kengai, Moyogi, Kabutachi

Shakan, 7 in (18 cm) height,
13¼ in (34 cm) width, Koyo pot

Red seeds bursting open, and a venerable trunk

It naturally grows from Hokkaido to Kyushu. When the fruits ripen, they rip open and red seeds fall one by one. In the fall, the leaves turn to yellow, then red and, finally, to a beautiful bright red color. Since it thickens easily, it easily ends up looking older.

ACTIVITY CALENDAR

Jan	Feb	Mar	Apr	May	Jun	Jul	Aug	Sep	Oct	Nov	Dec
		Transplanting	Transplanting								
			Sprout Plucking	Sprout Plucking	Sprout Plucking						
				Fertilizing	Fertilizing			Fertilizing	Fertilizing		
Wire placing/ removal	Wire placing/ removal	Wire placing/ removal	Wire placing/ removal	Wire placing/ removal							Wire placing/ removal

MANAGEMENT TIPS

Placement Place in a well-lit and well-ventilated area. In summer, avoid direct sunlight.

Watering When the surface of the soil is dry, give plenty of water. If given too much water, the chances of root rotting.

Fertilizing Give solid fertilizer.

Pest Damage Be careful of aphids and scale insects.

Transplanting Once every two years. Best done between March and April.

MAKING A KENGAI

Before: Mid-April

→

After: Mid-April

→

After: Mid-June

WIRING/BRANCH ARRANGING (MID-APRIL)

1 Wrap one branch at a time and arrange them.

2 Appearance after wiring and branch arranging are completed.

TRANSPLANTING (MID-APRIL)

1 Use a rake to scoop the roots downwards.

2 Cut the sides of the roots using rooting scissors.

3 Appearance after cutting the roots.

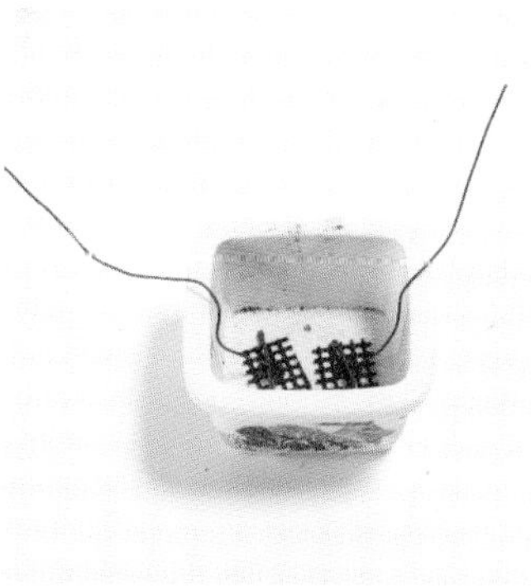

4 Prepare the pot and the lower soil (akadama medium 80%; river sand 20%).

※Use a mixture of 80% akadama medium grain, 20% river sand.

5 Appearance after transplanting is completed and moss has been spread.

MEMO

Tip for better fruiting

This is a hermaphrodite species. Flowers sprout on the tip of the newer and shorter branches. So when pruning, cut branches until they have only two sprouts left at most. Shortening the branches encourages more fruits. If left with other Nishikigi, it also grows better fruits.

Hankengai, 6 in (15 cm) height, 12 in (30 cm) width, Chinese-style pot

Sanzashi 山査子

PROFILE

OTHER NAMES Fruit Sanzashi, Flower Sanzashi
CLASS Rosaceae
TREE SHAPE Kengai, BunJingi, Moyogi, Shakan

Lovely small red fruits, also used as natural remedy

Originally from China, they were imported to Japan long ago. The red, multilayered flowers do not produce fruit, but the single, folded white flowers do produce fruit. The tree pictured here is a white flower variant. The red fruits can be appreciated until late February and can be processed for use in natural remedies or can be dried. Being very robust, this tree is recommended for beginners.

ACTION CALENDAR	Jan	Feb	Mar	Apr	May	Jun	Jul	Aug	Sep	Oct	Nov	Dec
Transplanting			■						■			
Fruiting	■											
Sprout plucking				■	■	■						
Fertilizing					■	■			■	■		
Wire placing/ removal	■	■	■		■							■

MANAGEMENT TIPS

Placement Place in a well-lit and well-ventilated area. In summer, it's essential to keep it in shade. However, this tree is strong to cold.

Watering When the surface of the soil is dry, give plenty of water. Make sure to not let it dry out during the flower blossoming period.

Fertilizing Give solid fertilizer.

Pest Damage Be careful of aphids and scale insects.

Transplanting Once every two years. Best done in March or September.

MAKING A HANKENGAI

Before: Late March

→

After: Late March

→

After: Mid-May

PRUNING (LATE MARCH)

1 Remove branches that ruin the overall shape of the tree using branch-cutting scissors.

TIP

Apply healing coating on the cuts.

2 Cut the branches going the opposite way compared to the flow of the tree shape with branch-cutting scissors.

3 Appearance after pruning.

TRANSPLANTING (LATE MARCH)

TIP

If the roots are bent, they'll be easier to scoop and, later, to loosen.

1 Cut the roots vertically using rooting scissors.

2 Scoop the roots downwards with a rake.

3 Appearance after scooping the roots.

4 Prepare the pot and the lower soil (akadama medium 80%; river sand 20%; add 10% of bamboo charcoal in the mix as well).

※Use a mixture of 80% akadama medium grain, 20% river sand, and add about 10% bamboo charcoal.

5 Appearance after the transplanting is completed and moss has been spread.

PRUNING (MID-MAY)

1 Appearance of grown branches.

2 Cut the longer branches using pruning scissors.

3 Appearance after pruning.

MEMO

Tip for better fruiting

In early June, artificially pollinate the larger and the smaller flowers. Being a hermaphrodite species, this tree can also self-breed naturally.

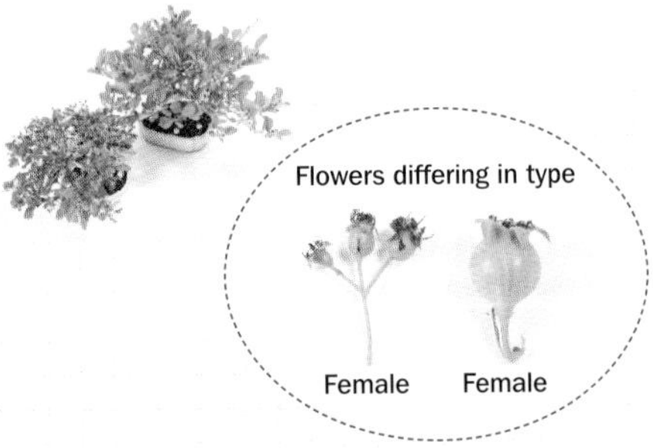

Tachibana Modoki

橘擬

Kabutachi, 6¼ in (16 cm) height, Eastern temple pot

PROFILE

OTHER NAMES Piracansa, Tokiwasanzatsu
CLASS Rosaceae
TREE SHAPE Kabutachi, Shakan, Moyogi, Kengai

Yellow-orange fruits, with thorns in both fruit and branches

Originally from Europe and Asia. This tree's scientific Japanese name is Pirakansa, and in the world of bonsai, Pirakansa is the name more often used. It comes from the Latin, meaning "thorns of fire." The branches are indeed thorny, so care is required when working on them. White flowers gather and bloom in early summer; if flowers bloom, the tree will certainly grow fruits later.

ACTION CALENDAR

Jan	Feb	Mar	Apr	May	Jun	Jul	Aug	Sep	Oct	Nov	Dec
	Transplanting										
	Leaf cutting										
			Sprout plucking								
			Fertilizing					Fertilizing			
	Wire placing/ removal										

MANAGEMENT TIPS

Placement Place in a well-lit and well-ventilated area. It's very resistant to heat and cold.

Watering When the surface of the soil is dry, give plenty of water.

Fertilizing Give solid fertilizer.

Pest Damage Be careful of aphids, scale insects and black spots.

Transplanting Once every two years. Best done between February and April.

TRANSPLANTING TO A SHALLOW POT

Before: Early November

→

Before: Mid-February

→

After: Mid-February

→

After: Mid-May

LEAF CUTTING (MID-FEBRUARY)

1 Cut leaves at their base using pruning scissors.

TIP

Leaves sprout in April. Cutting back leaves in winter promotes strong spring foliage.

2 Appearance after leaf cutting is completed.

PRUNING (MID-FEBRUARY)

1 Cut unnecessary and withering branches using pruning scissors.

2 Apply Coating healing agent with a spatula/hard brush to the cut wounds.

WIRING/BRANCH ARRANGING (MID-FEBRUARY)

TIP

Lowering the tip of the branches makes the tree look older.

1 Wrap one branch at a time and arrange the tip of the branches downwards.

TRANSPLANTING (MID-FEBRUARY)

1 Scoop the lower part of the roots with a rake.

2 Cut longer roots using rooting scissors.

3 Appearance of cut roots.

4 Prepare the pot and the lower soil (akadama medium grain, add 10% of bamboo charcoal to the mix).

※Use a mixture of 80% akadama medium grain, 20% river sand, and add about 10% bamboo charcoal.

5 Place the lower soil in the bottom of the pot.

6 Add the tree and the top layer of soil (akadama small grain 80%, river sand 20%).

TIP

Don't place the bamboo charcoal on the surface of the soil; it will float if you immerse the pot in water.

※Use a mixture of 80% akadama small grain, 20% river sand.

7 Use a bamboo spatula to make sure there are no gaps in the soil.

8 Bend the wire to fix the tree and cut the excess wire.

9 Immerse the entire pot in water until the top layer of soil is moist. This is done so that the soil can take in plenty of water. Allow to drain.

SPREADING A NET OVER THE WATER MOSS (MID-FEBRUARY)

1 Soak water moss in water and shape it into a string.

2 Place and spread on the soil using tweezers.

3 Push the water moss gently with your fingertips to fix it.

4 Bend thin metal wire in a U shape.

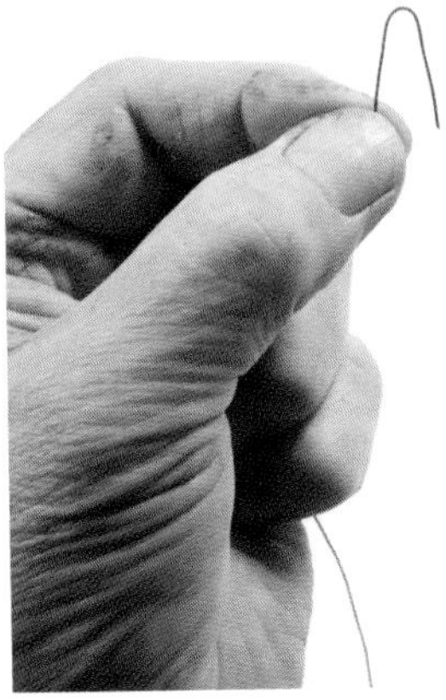

5 Cut the net to be around ⅜ in (1 cm) higher than the soil and fix it with the U-shaped wire from the previous step.

6 After stretching the net to the corners of the pot, fold it to cover the entire surface of the soil.

7 Appearance after transplanting is completed and both water moss and net have been placed.

8 In May, sprouts start to emerge.

MEMO

Tip for better fruiting

Flower buds grow on shorter branches then flower the next year. Ba careful not to cut the flower buds when pruning. This is a hermaphrodite species. It can produce good fruit naturally without any external help.

Kengai, 6 in (15 cm) height,
12 in (30 cm) width, Bigei pot

Tsuribana 吊花

PROFILE

OTHER NAMES Spindle tree
CLASS Celastraceae
TREE SHAPE Kengai, Hankengai, BunJingi

Fruits like wind chimes and an elegant narrow trunk

This grows throughout Japan. It's originally from temperate areas of China and Korea, but it is nonetheless very resistant to cold. It has red fruits that open; vermilion seeds hang down from the openings. They are very beautiful to see in soft wind. This tree is related to Mayumi and Komayumi, and the shape of their fruits is similar. Because the branches are few, arrange them so they follow the shape of the trunk.

ACTION CALENDAR

Jan	Feb	Mar	Apr	May	Jun	Jul	Aug	Sep	Oct	Nov	Dec
		Transplanting	Transplanting								
		Tree cutting	Tree cutting								
			Sprout plucking	Sprout plucking							
			Fertilizing	Fertilizing				Fertilizing	Fertilizing		
		Wire placing/ removal	Wire placing/ removal	Wire placing/ removal	Wire placing/ removal	Wire placing/ removal					

MANAGEMENT TIPS

Placement Place in a well-lit and well-ventilated area. In summer, it's essential to avoid direct sunlight.

Watering When the surface of the soil is dry, give plenty of water. Be careful not to water too much during the growing season.

Fertilizing Give solid fertilizer.

Pest Damage Be careful of aphids, scale insects and soot. Apply sterilizer periodically to prevent these issues.

Transplanting Once every two years. Best done in March or April.

TRANSPLANTING TO A SHALLOW POT

Before: Early November

→

After: Early April

→

After: Early April

→

After: Mid-May

PRUNING (EARLY APRIL)

1 Use pruning scissors to cut any branches that ruin the tree shape.

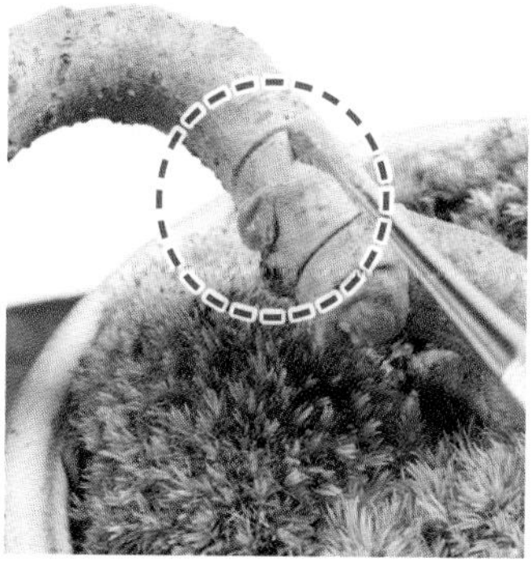

2 Apply healing protective coating to the cut wounds with a hard brush/spatula.

WIRING/BRANCH ARRANGING (EARLY APRIL)

1 Wrap one branch at a time and arrange them.

2 Appearance after wiring and branch arranging are completed.

TRANSPLANTING (EARLY APRIL)

1 Appearance of the tree after it's been removed from its original pot.

2 Prepare the new pot and the soil (akadama medium 80%; river sand 20%).

※Use a mixture of 80% akadama medium grain, 20% river sand.

3 Appearance after transplanting is completed and moss has been spread.

MEMO

Tip for better fruiting

This is a hermaphrodite species. In mid-May the flowers start blooming and the tree self-pollinates. Once June arrives, small fruits start to emerge and grow.

Tsuruume Modoki

蔓梅擬

Shakan, 4 in (10 cm) height,
6 in (15 cm) width, Shouseki round pot

PROFILE

OTHER NAMES Tsuru Modoki
CLASS Celastraceae
TREE SHAPE Kengai, Fukinagashi, Modoki, BunJingi, Neagari

With yellow split fruits, it's a vine that looks like an old tree

It's native to Japan and Korea. Yellow fruits split, letting the small vermilion seeds be seen from outside. Although it is a vine species, if grown for many years its trunk hardens and it starts looking like an old tree. The main charm of this species is the small branches, dividing and spreading into smaller branches. The change of the leaves from yellow to orange is also splendid. Its shape changes depending whether the roots are covered or not (in the case of Neagari).

ACTION CALENDAR	Jan	Feb	Mar	Apr	May	Jun	Jul	Aug	Sep	Oct	Nov	Dec
			Transplanting									
				Sprout Cutting								
				Fertilizing					Fertilizing			
			Wire placing						Wire removal			

MANAGEMENT TIPS

Placement Place in a well-lit and well-ventilated area. If left in shade, the fruits will be ruined. Move into partial shade during Rainy season (June) and summer.

Watering It likes water. When the surface of the soil is dry, give plenty of water. In summer, water 2–3 times a day.

Fertilizing Give solid fertilizer.

Pest Damage Be careful of aphids and scale insects.

Transplanting Once every two o years. Best done in March–April.

TRANSPLANTING TO A BONSAI POT

Before: Late April

After: Mid-June

WIRING/BRANCH ARRANGING (MID-APRIL)

1 Wrap one branch at a time and arrange them.

2 Appearance after wiring and branch arranging are completed.

TRANSPLANTING (LATE APRIL)

1 Use a rake to scoop the roots downwards.

2 Cut the longer roots using rooting scissors.

3 Appearance of roots after cutting the longer roots.

4 Spray the roots with high pressured water.

TIP

If you don't have an high pressure hose, pushing the tip of the hose also works fine.

5 Prepare the pot and the lower soil (akadama medium grain 80%; river sand 20%).

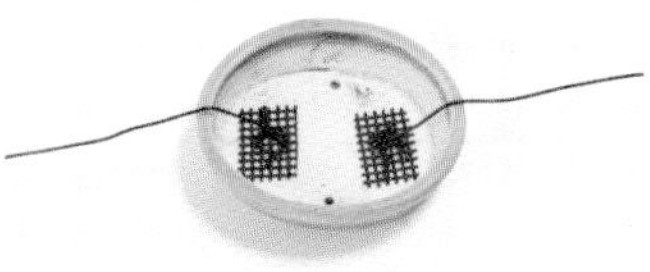

※Use a mixture of 80% akadama medium grain, 20% river sand.

6 Place the tree, apply the top layer of soil (akadama medium grain 80%; river sand 20%) and use tweezers to make sure there are no gaps in the soil.

7 Appearance after transplanting is completed and moss has been spread.

SPROUT CUTTING (MID-JUNE)

1 Appearance of grown sprouts.

2 Use pruning scissors to cut the grown sprouts.

MEMO

Tip for better fruiting

This tree breeds at the beginning of summer when the flowers start blooming. It's a hermaphrodite species. It can self-breed naturally, but we can improve the pollination by artificially taking the tip of the male flower and placing it on the female flower.

Binankazura 美男葛

PROFILE

OTHER NAMES Sanekazura, Sanakazura
CLASS Schisandraceae
TREE SHAPE Shakan, Moyogi, Kengai, Ishitsuki

Kengai, 8 in (20 cm) height, 10¼ in (26 cm) width, Chinese style pot

Red fruits grace this tree well into winter

Originally from Western Kanto, Korea and Taiwan. From bright white flowers it grows hanging red fruit clusters. The flowers bloom between August and September. Fruits start appearing in November, stay red until the end of December, changing to a light pink until February.

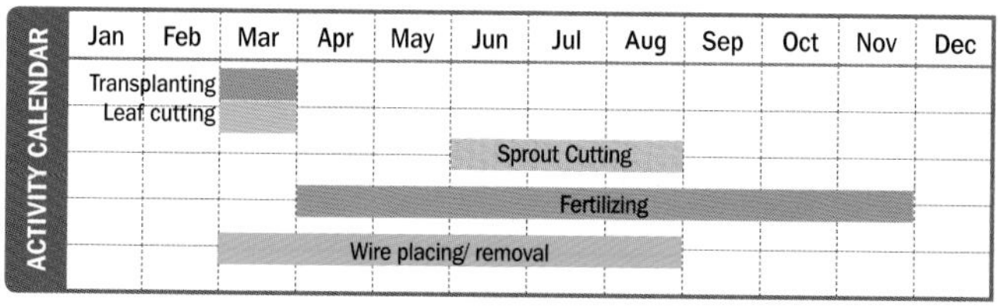

MANAGEMENT TIPS

Placement Place in a well-lit and well-ventilated area. It can also grow in partial shade, but this will decelerate branch growth.

Watering It likes water. When the surface of the soil is dry, give plenty of water.

Fertilizing Give solid fertilizer. If given plenty of fertilizer, the flower season will be longer, growing in a vine-like manner, which makes changing the tree shape easier.

Pest Damage It's immune to most damage.

Transplanting Once every year or two. Best done in March.

MAKING A KENGAI

Before: Early March

→

After: Early March

→

After: Mid-May

PRUNING (LATE MARCH)

1 Use pruning scissors to cut the overlapping branches.

2 Appearance after pruning.

WIRING/BRANCH ARRANGING (LATE MARCH)

1 Wrap one branch at a time and arrange them.

2 Appearance after wiring and branch arranging are completed.

TRANSPLANTING (LATE MARCH)

1 Cut the longer roots using rooting scissors.

2 Scoop and loosen the roots downwards with a rake.

3 Appearance after scooping the roots.

4 Fill a bucket with water and clean the roots with a tawashi (scrubbing brush).

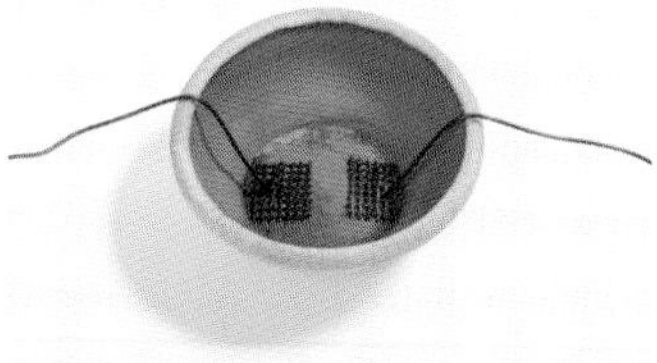

5 Prepare the pot and the lower soil (akadama medium 80%; river sand 20%. Add around 10% worth of bamboo charcoal and mix).

※Use a mixture of 80% akadama medium grain, 20% river sand, and add about 10% bamboo charcoal.

6 Appearance after transplanting is completed and moss has been spread.

SPROUT CUTTING (MID-JUNE)

1 Use pruning scissors to cut the grown sprouts.

MEMO

Tip for better fruiting

It is possible for both a female and a male flower to bloom from the same stump. Male flowers bloom in the early morning and have a very short lifespan, so refrigerate them and use them for artificial pollination.

Himeringo 姫林檎

Moyogi, 6 in (15 cm) height, Hideaki pot

PROFILE

OTHER NAMES Inuring, Mikaidou
CLASS Rosaceae
TREE SHAPE Moyogi, Shakan, Kengai

With beautiful red fruits, this is the Queen of Mimono Bonsai!

Originally from China, this tree grows naturally from Hokkaido to Hokuriku. It's a smaller apple tree species. Beautiful white flowers bloom in early summer and lead to bright red fruits in fall. It's truly the queen of bonsai. It is robust and simple to grow even for beginners; however, keep in mind that if grown from seeds, it won't produce any fruit.

ACTIVITY CALENDAR

<table>
<tr><th>Jan</th><th>Feb</th><th>Mar</th><th>Apr</th><th>May</th><th>Jun</th><th>Jul</th><th>Aug</th><th>Sep</th><th>Oct</th><th>Nov</th><th>Dec</th></tr>
<tr><td></td><td></td><td></td><td>Transplanting</td><td></td><td></td><td></td><td></td><td colspan="2">Transplanting</td><td></td><td></td></tr>
<tr><td></td><td></td><td></td><td></td><td></td><td></td><td></td><td></td><td></td><td></td><td colspan="2">Fruiting</td></tr>
<tr><td></td><td></td><td colspan="2">Fertilizing</td><td></td><td colspan="2">Fertilizing</td><td></td><td colspan="2">Fertilizing</td><td></td><td></td></tr>
<tr><td></td><td></td><td colspan="4">Wire placing/ removal</td><td></td><td></td><td></td><td></td><td></td><td></td></tr>
</table>

MANAGEMENT TIPS

Placement Place in a well-lit but dry area. In summer, avoid direct sunlight in late afternoon. In winter, move under cover.

Watering After pollination, make sure to not let it dry out.

Fertilizing Give solid fertilizer.

Pest Damage Be careful of black spot blight, chestnut blight, root carcinoma and aphids.

Transplanting Once every year. Best done in April or September–October.

MEMO

Tips for better fruiting

The flowers blossom in April. Fruits start to appear in May and reach their full growth in June.

1 For healthier fruits, avoid transplanting.
2 Artificially pollinate the female flowers (apples) with the male flowers.
3 After flowers start blooming, be careful not to expose the tree to rain. However, moving it indoors or leaving it under cover more than necessary will reduce the flow of pollen.

Blueberry ブルーベリー

PROFILE

OTHER NAMES Numasunoki
CLASS Ericaceae
TREE SHAPE Shakan, Fukinagashi

Fukinagashi, 6¾ in (17 cm) height,
10 in (25 cm) width, Japanese style pot

With small dark blue fruits, it also has beautiful red leaves in the fall

Said to be native to North America. It's cultivated in temperate areas all around the world. White bell-like flowers bloom in April. The fruits take their color in June, and in fall the leaves turn red. Being resistant to pest damage, there is no need to disinfect it and fruits are edible without requiring any further cleaning. Being an Ericacea, it is suitable for tree cutting and replanting.

ACTION CALENDAR

	Jan	Feb	Mar	Apr	May	Jun	Jul	Aug	Sep	Oct	Nov	Dec
Transplanting			■						■			
Fruiting					■	■						
Fertilizing			■	■		■	■		■	■		
Wire placing/ removal			■	■	■	■	■					

MANAGEMENT TIPS

Placement Place in a well-lit and well-ventilated area. If left in partial shade, the fruits will be ruined.

Watering It likes water. When the surface of the soil is dry, give plenty of water. In summer, water twice a day.

Fertilizing Give solid fertilizer.

Pest Damage It doesn't require care against pest damage.

Transplanting Once every two years. Best done in March or September.

MAKING A FUKINAGASHI

Before: Late March

→

After: Late March

PRUNING (LATE MARCH)

1 Use branch-cutting scissors to cut unnecessary standing branches

WIRING/BRANCH ARRANGING (LATE MARCH)

1 Wrap one branch at a time and arrange them.

2 Appearance after wiring and branch arranging are completed.

TRANSPLANTING (LATE MARCH)

1 Scoop the roots downwards with a rake, cut the longer roots using rooting scissors, then scoop and loosen the roots again.

2 Use wire to wrap the roots that stand up, and orient them downwards.

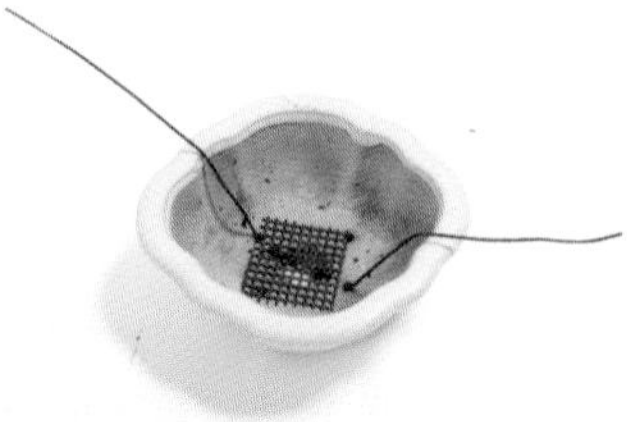

3 Prepare the pot and the soil (akadama small grain 75%; kanuma soil 25%).

※Use a mixture of 75% akadama small grain, 25% kanuma soil.

4 Appearance after transplanting is completed and water moss has been spread.

MEMO

Tip for better fruiting

Flowers start to blossom in early April. In early June, once the blueberries take on their color, they can be eaten. Picking the fruit is necessary because this species is too productive. Give plenty of fertilizer.

Beni Shitan 紅紫檀

PROFILE

OTHER NAMES Rock cotoneaster
CLASS Rosaceae
TREE SHAPE Shakan, Kengai, Moyogi, Yoseue

Shakan, 6 in (15 cm) height, 7 in (18 cm) width,
Japanese-style pot

Bright red, round fruits, and the tree shape can be arranged freely

Originally from China, this tree was exported first to Europe, then to Japan. It is a representative of Mimono. Many pink flowers bloom in spring. In September, the red fruits reach their full color and can be appreciated until the end of November. The variant with white flowers is called "Shiro Shitan." Being robust and being full of sprouts, it looks aged and can be arranged in plenty of shapes.

ACTION CALENDAR

Jan	Feb	Mar	Apr	May	Jun	Jul	Aug	Sep	Oct	Nov	Dec
		Transplanting									
				Sprout Cutting							
			Fertilizing		Fertilizing			Fertilizing			
		Wire placing/ removal									

MANAGEMENT TIPS

Placement Place in a well-lit and well-ventilated area. In summer, avoid direct sunlight, in winter, move under cover.

Watering Be careful to not let it dry out during growth periods and in summer.

Fertilizing Give solid fertilizer.

Pest Damage It's not weak to any particular pest damage.

Transplanting Once every two years. Best done between March and April.

TRANSPLANTING TO A POT THAT MATCHES THE TREE SHAPE

Before: Early November

→

Before: Late March

→

After: Late March

→

After: Mid-June

PRUNING (LATE MARCH)

1 Use pruning scissors to cut the branches pointing downward.

TIP

Making the lower outline of the branches more defined vastly improves the tree shape.

WIRING/BRANCH ARRANGING (LATE MARCH)

1 Wrap one branch at a time and arrange them.

2 Appearance after wiring and branch arranging are completed.

TRANSPLANTING (LATE MARCH)

1 Use a rake to scoop the roots downwards.

2 Cut the longer roots using rooting scissors.

3 Appearance after cutting the roots.

4 Prepare the pot and the bottom soil (akadama medium 80%; river sand 20%, add 10% of bamboo charcoal into the mix).

※Use a mixture of 80% akadama medium grain, 20% river sand, and add about 10% bamboo charcoal.

5 Appearance after transplanting is completed and moss has been spread.

SPROUT CUTTING (MID-JUNE)

1 Appearance of grown sprouts.

2 Use pruning scissors to cut the grown sprouts.

WIRING/BRANCH ARRANGING (MID-JUNE)

1 Wrap the new branch tips one branch at a time and arrange them.

2 Appearance after wiring and branch arranging are completed.

MEMO

Tip for better fruiting

Flowers bloom in April and immediately grow fruits. If flowers bloom, fruits will certainly appear; artificial pollination is not necessary.

Mayumi 真弓

Hankengai, 4 in (10 cm) height, Tofukuji pot

PROFILE

OTHER NAMES Tamatebako, Saru no juubako, Mikono-suzu, Ichikomasu.
CLASS Celastraceae
TREE SHAPE Shakan, Kengai, Bunjingi, Moyogi

Fruits like wind chimes and a trunk with a look of antiquity

It grows in mountains everywhere in Japan. It is a tree with large fruits, which makes it valuable. Light green flowers start blooming in early summer. In fall the temporary pale scarlet seeds split and the red seeds can be seen inside. There are also variants in which the temporary seeds are red or white. The tree pictured here is a variant with a rough type of bark, and is disposed to having a thicker trunk. It is recommended to frequently cut the trunk and cover the roots.

ACTION CALENDAR

	Jan	Feb	Mar	Apr	May	Jun	Jul	Aug	Sep	Oct	Nov	Dec
Transplanting			■									
Sprout plucking				■	■	■	■					
Fertilizing				■	■				■	■		
Wire placing/ removal					■	■	■					

MANAGEMENT TIPS

Placement Place in a well-lit and well-ventilated area. In winter, move under cover.

Watering It likes water. When the surface of the soil is dry, give plenty of water. Be careful to not let it dry out during summer.

Fertilizing Give solid fertilizer. If not given enough fertilizer, the fruits might fall off the tree.

Pest Damage Be careful of aphids. Take counter mea-sures against birds

Transplanting Once every two years. Best done in March.

TRANSPLANTING TO A POT THAT MATCHES THE TREE SHAPE

Before: Early November

→

Before: Early March

→

After: Early March

WIRING/BRANCH ARRANGING (EARLY MARCH)

1 Wrap one branch at a time and arrange them.

2 Appearance after wiring and branch arranging are completed.

TIP

By doing this we bring branches closer to the trunk. By passing the wire through a rubber tube, we prevent damange to the trunk.

3 Pass a wire through a rubber tube and fix it to the trunk, then hook it to the branch wires.

TRANSPLANTING (LATE MARCH)

1 Appearance of the roots after they have been cut.

2 Prepare the pot and the soil (akadama medium 80%, river sand 20%, add around 10% worth of bamboo charcoal to the mix).

※Use a mixture of 80% akadama medium grain, 20% river sand, and add about 10% bamboo charcoal.

3 Appearance after transplanting is completed and the moss has been spread.

MEMO

Tip for better fruiting

Blooming starts in mid-May. Before pollination do not water the leaves. If watered, the male flowers will fall. Use tweezers or pruning scissors to remove the male pistil and place it on the female flower (photo on the left). Alternatively you can also place the full male flowers on top of female flowers (photo on the right) For watering, in order to avoid losing pollen, fill a bucket with water and let the soil receive the water through the bottom of the pot.

Female flowers: Middle is hollow. Male flowers: Pistils grow long.

Moyogi, 4¼ in (11 cm) height, Oyama pot

Miyamakaidou 深山海棠

PROFILE

OTHER NAMES Zumi, Kaidou
CLASS Rosaceae
TREE SHAPE Shakan, Moyogi, Kengai

Yellow or scarlet fruits and easy-to-arrange branches

Native to the mountains and fields of Northern Honshu to Hokkaido. This tree produces lovely yellow or scarlet fruits. Flowers only bud on shorter branches so it's important to be diligent about pruning. The fruits take their color around December and last until March. Small branches often diverge, making it easier to arrange them in any desired shape.

ACTION CALENDAR

	Jan	Feb	Mar	Apr	May	Jun	Jul	Aug	Sep	Oct	Nov	Dec
Transplanting			■									
Sprout plucking				■	■	■	■					
Fertilizing					■	■	■					
Wire placing/ removal			■	■	■	■	■					

MANAGEMENT TIPS

Placement Place in a well-lit and well-ventilated area. In winter, move indoors.

Watering It likes water. When the surface of the soil is dry, give plenty of water. Be careful to not let it dry out in summer.

Fertilizing Give solid fertilizer.

Pest Damage Be careful of aphids, scale insects and root carcinoma.

Transplanting Once every two years. Best done in March.

Memo

Trick for improving fruiting

As it's a hermaphrodite species, it doesn't require artificial pollination. Because Kaidou and apple trees are related, Kaidou pollen is often used for artificially pollinating apple trees.

Hankengai, 5¼ in (13 cm) height, Koyo pot

Rouyagaki 老爺柿

PROFILE

OTHER NAMES Tsukubanegaki
CLASS Ebenaceae
TREE SHAPE Shakan, Bunjingi, Kengai, Fukinagashi, Moyogi.

Big, glossy fruits conjure images of the fields in fall

This tree is originally from China. Fruits will be ⅜–¾ in (1–2 cm) long, and glossy orange or pink in color. Fruits grow in a bell shape and although they are sparse, they look splendid nevertheless. The variant pictured here is called "You Kihi." Its fruits get their color in September and last until February or March.

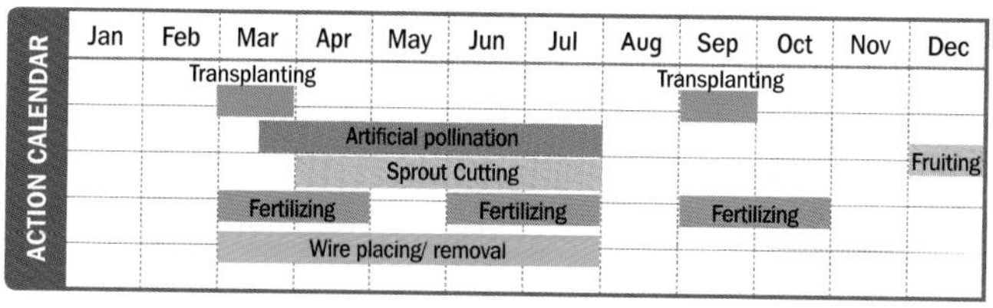

MANAGEMENT TIPS

Placement Place in a well-lit and well-ventilated area. During rainy season move under cover. Avoid direct sunlight in summer.

Watering When the surface of the soil is dry, give plenty of water. If left without water, the fruits might drop.

Fertilizing Give solid fertilizer. If given plenty, the flowers and fruits will be better.

Pest Damage Be careful of aphids and scale insects.

Transplanting Once every two years. Best done in March or September.

MAKING A HANKENGAI

Before: Late March

→

After: Late March

→

After: Mid-May

PRUNING (LATE MARCH)

1 Cut withering branches with branch-cutting scissors.

2 Cut branches that are either too long or ruin the overall shape of the tree with branch-cutting scissors.

WIRING/BRANCH ARRANGING (LATE MARCH)

1 Wrap one branch at a time and arrange them.

2 Use branch-cutting scissors to cut off the branches that ruin the flow of the tree.

3 Appearance after cutting the branches.

4 Appearance after wiring, arranging and pruning are completed.

TRANSPLANTING (LATE MARCH)

1 Replant the plant as it is.

TIP

Gaki roots contain astringent juice, which is why the roots are black in color.

2 Appearance after transplanting is completed and moss has been spread.

SPROUT CUTTING (MID-MAY)

1 Appearance of grown sprouts.

2 Use pruning scissors to cut the grown sprouts.

3 Appearance after sprouts are cut.

MEMO

Tips for better fruiting

POLLINATION

Artificially pollinate the flowers once they bloom. Take the tip of the male flowers and place it on female flowers.

Female flower:
Has calyx

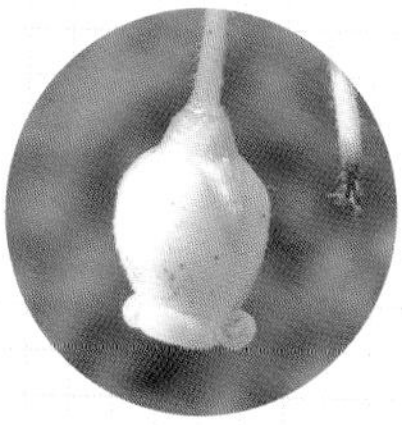

Male flower:
Doesn't have calyx

Fruits will grow in May. At this time the fruits will be bright green. However when getting closer to the fall, the fruits will change to a scarlet color.

SPRAY GIBBERELLIN

If flowers do not bloom, follow this method to encourage blooming.

If you use a spray bottle to apply Gibberellin (1 cap per 10 oz [300 ml] of water) on the flowers, the fruits will grow well and healthy.

Iwachidori 岩千鳥

4¾ in (12 cm) height, Chinese pot.

Sweet like a bird, with purple or white flowers

Originally from Western Honshu and Shihoku rocky areas. It's also called Yachiyo. Place in a well-lit and well-ventilated spot. Once the rainy season (June) begins, move it to partial shade so that leaves aren't damaged. Move back to direct sunlight in September. In the fall, once the upper part loses its shape, move to shade. Give plenty of water. To fertilize, use herb fertilizer in spring, and when sprouts emerge around early June and between mid-September and mid-October, give liquid fertilizer. Be careful of aphids and cabbage moths. Transplanting is done once a year in March, before sprouts emerge.

Perennial plant. Flowers bloom between late April and mid-May.

Kokemomo 苔桃

2 in (5 cm) height, Japanese pot.

Appreciated as a Mimono, with small flowers and red fruits

Originally from North America and Northern Europe. The original species is also called Lingonberry or Cowberry. The glossy leaves do not fall can be appreciated even in winter. It likes to be under direct sunlight. Give plenty of water once the surface of the soil is dry, and water twice a day in summer. Fertilizer is not really necessary but it's given once in spring and once in fall. There is no need to worry about pest damage. Transplanting is done once every 3–4 years and is best done between December and March.

Perennial plant. Flowers bloom between June and July. Harvesting is done in September and October.

2¼ in (6 cm) height, Tsuchi pot.

Sakurasou 桜草

Plenty of flowers ranging in color and shapes, going from light pink to white

This is a species native to Eastern Siberia, Northern China, Korea and Japan. Keep under sunlight and in a well-ventilated place from February to May. Between summer and fall, the leaves may turn yellow. If this occurs, move the plant to a colder place. Give plenty of water once the surface of the soil is dry. Give slow/mild fertilizer in a small quantity after transplanting.
In March and April, use diluted liquid fertilizer to improve the growth of flowers and grass. Be careful of cabbage moths and aphids. Transplanting is done between December and February; once every year or two we also do stump splitting.

Perennial plant. Flowers bloom between April and May.

2¼ in (6 cm) height, Tsuchi pot.

Sumire 菫

Quietly blooming on the roadside, this is the much-loved common Violet

Commonly found in grassland, fields, roadsides, backyards and many other places. It is a cold-resistant deciduous species and is often used to garnish bonsai. Place in a well-lit, humid area. To avoid leaf burns, move to partial shade during summer. Give plenty of water once the surface of the soil is dry. To fertilize, give slow/mild fertilizer for the first fertilization, then use liquid fertilizer 2–3 times a month from February to October. Be careful of powdery mildew and aphids. Transplanting is done once a year, either between late summer and late fall or between February and March.

Perennial plant. Flowers bloom between April and May.

3¼ in (8 cm) height, Japanese pot.

Daimonjizou 大文字草

Its flowers come in many colors and shapes

It's a common type of grass growing in rocky areas. Grow in a humid area in partial shade to improve flower quality. In winter, the part of the plant above the soil loses its shape, but if moved indoors in fall it can be appreciated for a long time. Give plenty of water when the surface of the soil is dry. In spring and after blooming give plenty of solid fertilizer. Be careful of cabbage moths. Transplanting is done after the flowers bloom in early spring.

Perennial plant. Flowers bloom between late April and mid-May

4¾ in (12 cm) height, Japanese pot.

Tanchousou 丹頂草

Many small flowers growing on stem tips

Originally from Northern China and Korea. It usually grows on hilly riversides. At the end of fall the part above the soil loses its shape. Place in a well-lit and well-ventilated spot. Avoid direct sunlight in summer. Give plenty of water when the surface of the soil is dry. A small amount of solid fertilizer is enough. Transplanting is done once every two or three years years during winter.

Perennial plant. Flowers bloom between February and March.

2 in (5 cm) height, Issou pot.

Tokiwahimehagi 常盤姫萩

Legume-like unusual flowers

Native to the Alps in Central Europe. Place in a well-lit, well-ventilated spot and avoid direct sunlight in summer. Give small amounts of solid fertilizer in March, May and October. There is no need to worry about pest damage. Transplanting is done between early February and late March or between late September and late October. Don't use acidic soil.

Evergreen Bush, Flowers bloom between April and June

3¼ in (8 cm) height, Hidekuni pot.

Nokongiku 野紺菊

Quietly blooming in fields during fall

This grows on mountains all over Japan. It's also known as Nogiku (Asteroidae). Place in a well-lit and well-ventilated spot. Avoid direct sunlight in summer. Give plenty of water. In April, May and September use solid fertilizer. Be careful of red spider mites and aphids. Transplant once every year or two in spring. Stock splitting can also be done.

Perennial plant. Flowers bloom between July and October.

2¼ in (6 cm) height, Katsuyama pot.

Himeyabukouji 姫藪柑子

Known for its sparse red fruits

It normally grows on forest floors. Place in a well-ventilated place and keep in shade from May to September, in partial shade in April and October, and under sunlight from November to March. In winter make sure it doesn't freeze. Be careful of aphids. Transplanting is done once every 2–3 years; the best time is either from February to April or from September to November.

2 in (5 cm) height, Issou pot.

Yukinoshita 雪の下

Bright flowers covered by white rings

It grows in mountainous and humid areas in Japan and China. Keep in shade or partial shade and avoid direct sunlight. It likes water. Give solid fertilizer in a moderate amount in spring and fall. Be careful of spider mites, aphids and cabbage moths. Since the parent spike tips wither after flowering, once the flowers bloom, take the tips of the new bulbs and plant them in a new pot.

BONSAI AS PART OF YOUR INTERIOR DECOR

The bonsai you have put so much love into deserves to be admired. This doesn't have to be an expensive project. Pots can be found at dollar stores, thrift shops and similar. You can put your bonsai in the entrance of your home or in your living room. You only need some space and a few ideas, and you are good to go!

Decor: Kamakura by Narimatsu Sachie (Yamato Gardening Association)

Cat paw tables

Having some height difference when lining up two plants adds a three-dimensional effect. It improves the overall balance.

Image: Komochiiwarenge (left) and Inzanshou (right)

❖ Place on a bamboo mat and coasters

Try using pastel coasters or flat plates, placed on a textured surface like this bamboo mat.

Image: (left) Tokiwashinobu and Himegiboushi (right)

❖ Using shelves and stools

Jazz it up with shelves to add rhythm. When you place the bonsai in a triangle formation, the look somehow becomes balanced. Figurines make a nice accent.

Images clockwise from top: Kaede, Kakushimasusuki and Shikushikaramatsusou

TERMS USED IN BONSAI

Accent/accessory plants This refers to miscellaneous trees, flowers, fruits and grasses included with a main tree to form an arrangement. The terms "accents" and "accessories" also pertain to stones and other embellishments.

Accompaniments Small objects such as ceramic people and animals, sea creatures, bridges and so on. When arranged with bonsai, narrative is born.

Additional fertilization Do this during a tree's growing season.

Adventitious bud Normally, trees shoot near the side of the leaves. This is a bud that grows from an unusual place such as the middle of the trunk and branches.

Age Length of a tree's life from seedling to present. In the case of bonsai, it may be judged by the condition of the bark.

Agrobacterium tumefaciens A disease that causes tumors to form on roots and stems of many types of plants. It occurs easily in bonsai of the rose family. Sterilize the roots when replanting in order to prevent this.

Akadama soil Soil used in bonsai. Available in small and medium grain, retains water well while also providing good drainage.

Apex The highest point of the tree.

Apical A tree's most vigorous growth, most frequently the outer branches.

Artificial pollination Pollinating by placing pollen on stamen and pistil.

Bamboo charcoal Soil additive made by baking bamboo at extremely high temperatures. It helps neutralize soil, takes in water and nutrients well, and has good drainage.

Basic tree form A tree's fundamental shape—the starting point for creating beautiful bonsai.

Black spot A fungal disease characterized by black spots or patches on leaves. Watering facilitates its spread to other parts of the plant, so be sure to remove infected leaves before watering.

Bottom hole A hole in the bottom of the bonsai pot. The number of holes varies depending on the size and shape of the pot. These openings are needed for drainage.

Branch Primary branches are those growing directly from the trunk. Secondary branches grow from primary branches, tertiary branches grow from secondary branches, and so on. The lowest branch is considered the first branch, and subsequent branches are numbered upwards.

Broadleaf plants Plants whose leaves are flat and broad, such as the maple.

Bud branch Unwanted branches that disrupt a tree's shape. If you find one during pruning, be sure to remove it.

Bud break State in which a bud's green tip has opened up enough to be visible.

Bud burst Point at which new leaves have begun to unfurl.

Bud picking The tip of the sprout is picked with forceps in order to promote the growth of side sprouts.

BunJingi bonsai Also called Literati, this tree shape features a thin trunk that is stretched, sometimes contorted, and has no lower branches. Branches and leaves are sparse and confined to the top.

Buttress The surface roots (see Nebari). Also called root flare.

Callus Healing tissue that grows over a wound on a branch or trunk.

Colored pot Pot that is glazed in a color.

Conifer Cone-bearing trees, such as the pine and the larch.

Crown Upper part of the tree beginning at the point where branches spread out from the trunk.

Cultivar Basically, a plant that has been grown through selection and breeding, rather than growing naturally in the wild.

Cut/wound/healing paste For painting on the cut end of the trunk after pruning so as to close it. It prevents bacteria from entering from the incision.

Cutting A breeding method by which branches are cut from a donor tree and placed in soil.

Deadwood techniques Techniques such as downing branches, exposing stripped trunks or branches to elements, and thick rooting to give the appearance of antiquity or disguise flaws in a bonsai.

Debranching Reducing the number of branches to avoid crowding and achieve balance.

Deciduous plants Plants whose leaves shed in the fall and form anew in the spring. Maples and elms are examples of deciduous bonsai.

Deep pot Generally higher than they are wide, often used for cliff (cascades) and half-cliff (half-cascade) bonsai shapes.

Defoliating Removing a tree's leaves in summer to force new growth.

Dessication A state of thorough dryness.

Dieback Death of new growth due to disease, pests or conditions.

Display shelf There are several types of shelves made specifically for bonsai display. Most often, these contain two or three tiers.

Dwarfism When a cultivar or variety is smaller than the species tree, but otherwise retains the all of the tree's characteristics.

Ear The grain-bearing tip of the stem of a cereal plant.

Evergreen plants Plants that are green year-round.

Fertilizing Feeding your bonsai during its growth season, utilizing granular or liquid fertilizer containing the nutrients nitrogen, potassium and kalium. Needs are determined by such factors as species and the age of the tree. Check the fertilization guidelines for your specific bonsai before taking this important step.

Flower buds As with other flowering plants, bonsai flower buds blossom into flowers after growth. Depending on the tree species, flower buds may be attached differently, so care must be taken when pruning.

Flower carcass A flower that has finished blooming. If left unchecked, the trees may become weak and the deadened bloom could cause a mold problem. It is important to remove dead flowers carefully and regularly.

Four seasons bloomer A flower that blooms all year long.

Fukinagash (windswept) A bonsai shape in which a trunk or branch seems to be blowing in heavy wind.

Grafting In bonsai, grafting consists of transferring a branch to a bare part of the tree so as to produce new growth by connecting the tissue of branch to stem/trunk.

Grass plants A classification of bonsai. There are many grass plants that will flower, such as mountain wild grass. It is often used as accent in bonsai arrangement.

Gray mold A quickly-spreading fungal disease that appears as mushy gray spots on leaves, stems, flowers and fruits. It is exacerbated by high humidity.

Gymnosporangium Genus of fungi that produce yellowish/rusty depressions on the leaves. It infects various types of trees. It is particularly harmful to fruit-bearing types.

Hankengai (half-cliff/half-cascade) Like the Kengai (cliff/cascade), a bonsai shape in which the trunk and branches hang low, often over the edge of the pot.

Hermaphrodite plants Plants with both male and female reproductive properties. They are self-fertilizing.

Heterosexual plants Plants that are either male or female.

Hikobae Also called Yagome. This is an adventitious shoot that sprouts at the foot of a tree. If left alone, it will cause the original tree to weaken, so if you find one of these, remove it.

Hiraishi A natural stone that can be used as a container for bonsai. Use keto soil to aid in adhesion. This stone can be found in various tones and shapes, some with cracks, which can produce a sense of age.

Hokidachi (broom style) A good style for deciduous trees, this bonsai shape features a straight trunk from which branches grow in all directions, forming a rounded crown.

Immersion/soaking Sinking the bonsai pot in a basin of water, a method to be used only as first aid, in cases where the soil is very dry and compact, or for plants whose roots extend to the extremities of the pot. This allows the plant to drink in water through the bottom of the pot.

Ishitsuki Bonsai shape that gives the impression of trees clinging to rocks or cliffs. A shallow pot allows for a strong rocky landscape, while a deeper pot allows for a close intermingling of smaller rocks with the trees' roots.

Jin Deadwood technique in which bark is stripped away from branch, to simulate age and exposure to elements.

Kabudachi A tree with multiple trunks growing from a single root.

Kanuma soil Soil commonly used for Ericaceous (acid loving) bonsai types such as Satsuki.

Kengai (cliff/cascade) Bonsai shape in which the trunk and branches hang low, often over the edge of the pot.

Keto soil A clay-like soil used for various bonsai purposes, including creating adhesion to rocks.

Kokedama A form of bonsai in which a plant's roots are grown in a ball of soil covered in moss.

Large bonsai Size category for bonsai trees that can reach up to 40 inches (approximately 100 cm) in height

Layering Ground layering is a propagation method that uses branches to produce roots by allowing the adventitious buds of a heavily-laden (ground-touching) branch to touch the soil in order to root. In air layering, wire may be wrapped around trunk or branch to slow the flow of nutrients and force buds to form above the wire (tourniquet method) or stripping a ring of bark down to the hard wood and wrapping the ring with sphagnum moss and plastic (ring method).

Leader Main shoot of the branch, found at the top. The branch's growth extends from this shoot.

Leaf burn This state is evident when leaves and branches turn brown or yellow in summer. It is often caused by summer runoff. Depending on the tree species, it is also important to shade your bonsai.

Leaf reduction Removal of leaves to maintain a tree's balance. Also refers to the state of leaf reduction attained through pruning and defoliating.

Leaf watering When watering, water the leaves. This is a good practice on a hot summer day or immediately after replanting.

Leafiness Pertaining to the size, shape and density of a bonsai's leaves. Depending on the tree genus, even the similar species may have different leaf characteristics. Thin leaves, short ones, dense ones, different shades, etc. Each tree species has an ideal leafiness.

Leafing trimming/pruning To thin out crowded leaves and remove dead ones. This improves circulation and photosynthesis.

Lignification This pertains to the condition and appearance of a tree's wood—its texture and look of maturity or antiquity.

Liquid fertilizer Generally nitrogen-rich fertilizer in liquid form. It is fast-acting and can be used in various ways. Always follow manufacturer's directions.

Lotus mouth Watering can style in which the mouth releases a shower rather than a stream of water. This weaker water flow greatly reduces the chance of damage to trees.

Main tree The central tree in a grove or coppice. Alternatively, a tree (such as a pinewood) that takes the leading role in a bonsai arrangement.

Main trunk In plants that have multiple trunks, this is the central/base trunk.

Mame bonsai Class of small bonsai that reach only about 4 inches (10 cm) in height.

Medium bonsai Bonsai in this category grow anywhere from 10–36 inches (about 25–92 cm).

Miscellaneous trees A term for trees falling outside the representative types that can be raised as or with bonsai.

Moss sprinkling/scattering Cutting tips of moss and scattering on the soil in order to propagate new moss. The new moss will grow uniformly and is finished cleanly.

Moyogi bonsai Bonsai shape also called the informal upright style, in which the trunk grows upright but curved, and branching occurs on all sides.

Nebari These are the surface roots. They create a visual balance between crown and base and are a special aspect of bonsai.

Node Point on a trunk or branch from which new buds, leaves or shoots emerge.

One-year-old breed Seedlings, cuttings, etc., from which flowering and fruiting can be expected within the first year.

Order of the trunk The trunk gradually tapers from the root to the crown. It is an important element to express the sense of large, fully grown trees.

Painted pot A pot to which paint has been applied to add color or decoration. Many design elements are painted over glaze.

Parent tree Tree whose branches are used for cutting and joining.

Partial shade This amounts to about three hours of sunlight daily, and avoiding western exposure.

Perennial plant A plant living two or more years.

Pinching back Carefully pulling off new shoots to maintain tree shape.

Pot bottom netting Use wire to affix this netting over the drainage holes from the inside of the pot. It prevents soil from flowing out and prevents insects from entering through the drainage holes.

Pot-bound plant A plant whose roots now fill the pot, leaving no room for expansion or for air circulation.

Powdery mildew A fungal disease characterized by white spots on leaves, usually prevalent in spring and fall.

Pruning Cutting back branches, leaves and trunk in order to maintain a healthy shape, remove dead branches, provide ventilation and avoid density that prevents light from reaching the branches.

Ramification Splitting of trunk and/or branches to form smaller ones.

Root pruning/trimming Trimming the roots of pot-bound plants to encourage new root growth and facilitate repotting.

Red leaves Leaves turning red in fall.

Reform To make major changes to bonsai tree shapes and the front of trees.

Replanting Transferring the bonsai from one pot to another, usually using fresh soil and treating/trimming the roots in the process.

Repotting To replant bonsai into another bonsai pot without using root treatment and using new soil.

River sand Soil consisting of particles of shell and/or rock. Used in bonsai for its good drainage properties.

Root washing When replanting, remove old soil and wash roots with water.

Rootstock Root system and stem onto which a new plant may be grafted (see also scion).

Rough skin A feature of some bonsai, popular because of the sense of antiquity that it lends even to younger trees.

Sabamiki A deadwood technique by which the trunk is divided, first through stripping the bark, then through creating deep wound to create and encourage a split.

Sacrifice branch A side branch allowed to grow out in order to encourage a thicker trunk. Wire the branch away from the trunk, and remove the branch at the appropriate time.

Sashieda The directional branch that serves as a tree's focal point. Factors such as the tree's height, the thickness of its trunk and so on determine which branch has this role, as balance is always extremely important in bonsai.

Saikei A bonsai arrangement generally planted on a dish a tray (often, a dish containing no drainage holes, called a suiban) to simulate a rocky landscape.

Scion Plant or portion of stem grafted onto a rootstock in order to propagate a new plant. The new plant will have the characteristics of the scion.

Seed tree A tree that is left in its habitat in order to provide seeds for natural regeneration.

Seishi After hooking, bending the branches freely to approximate the ideal tree shape.

Separately blooming Flower of various colors blooming in one tree.

Shade cloth Mesh fabric used to protect against cold and excessive sun. Can be stretched over wooden framing to filter sunlight.

Shading A means of shielding plants from summer light and high temperature, such as using shade cloth, or planting reeds to create an optimal environment for trees.

Shakan Bonsai shape in which the trunk leans to the right or left.

Shallow pot Pot whose depth is smaller than its opening.

Shari A deadwood technique that involves inflicting a small wound on the trunk and peeling back some of the bark.

Shohin Bonsai in the small (bordering on miniature) size rage. Also called "palm bonsai," as they can generally fit in the palm of a hand.

Short leaf method A pruning method unique to pines, and refers to shoot pinching, shoot cutting, sprouting and so on. This is done to keep leaves and branches short.

Sokan (double stem/trunk) Bonsai tree form in which the trunk may be split into two from the root.

Solid fertilizer Pelleted, granular and other non-liquid forms of fertilizer. These are long-and-slow-acting compared to liquid fertilizer.

Stem skin The condition of the surface of the trunk. The appearance differs depending on the tree, from smooth, to ragged, to peeled or stripped. In bonsai, surfaces that give the appearance of wood are highly appreciated.

Stock splitting To separate and the offspring from the plant's parent and then transplant.

Straight root A thick, long root that extends straight. In the case of bonsai, if you cut it early, the horizontal roots will grow and you will have a strong rooting.

Straight stem Bonsai tree shape with an upright trunk.

Sucker Shoot growing from the base of a plant.

Symbiotic bacteria Bacteria that have a mutually beneficial relationship with one another or with another organism. When replanting pine mushroom and similar, remove the root from the pot and you can see white areas around the root. These are an example of mycorrhizal fungi.

Table In the case of bonsai display, a four-legged stand.

Tanuki A technique that affixes young plant life onto dead wood.

Torsion stem A condition by which a stem is twisted to make the wood appear aged. A stem can be trained to twist by winding a wire around it.

Tree height Height from the rim of the pot to the apex of the tree.

Tree Shape A tree's form, including the manner of its trunk (e.g., upright or cascaded, number of stems), the shape formed by its branches, and so on.

Unglazed pot Unglazed pots are good choices for bonsai such as pines. An example of unglazed clay pots is the traditional Yixing ware (also called Zisha) which, while generally referred to as "purple clay," can vary in color.

Uro An indentation in a trunk that is formed when a branch rots and falls. This is also a deadwood technique in which a branch is removed to form an uro.

Wire hook Used for wiring trunk and branches. Once wired, the bonsai settles and prepares to take on its tree form. In bonsai, copper wire and aluminum wire are used.

Yellow leaves Leaves turning yellow in fall.

Yoseue (combined planting) A bonsai style in which several trees are planted in a single pot.

ALPHABETICAL LIST OF PLANTS

"Books to Span the East and West"

Tuttle Publishing was founded in 1832 in the small New England town of Rutland, Vermont [USA]. Our core values remain as strong today as they were then—to publish best-in-class books which bring people together one page at a time. In 1948, we established a publishing office in Japan—and Tuttle is now a leader in publishing English-language books about the arts, languages and cultures of Asia. The world has become a much smaller place today and Asia's economic and cultural influence has grown. Yet the need for meaningful dialogue and information about this diverse region has never been greater. Over the past seven decades, Tuttle has published thousands of books on subjects ranging from martial arts and paper crafts to language learning and literature—and our talented authors, illustrators, designers and photographers have won many prestigious awards. We welcome you to explore the wealth of information available on Asia at **www.tuttlepublishing.com.**

Published by Tuttle Publishing, an imprint of Periplus Editions (HK) Ltd.

ISBN 978-4-8053-1502-6

www.tuttlepublishing.com

ICHIBAN TEINEI NA HAJIMETE NO BONSAI NO SODATEKATA

English translation rights arranged with NIHONBUNGEI-SHA Co., Ltd. through Japan UNI Agency, Inc., Tokyo

PRODUCTION STAFF
Book design Gobo design office
Photography Kaneko Yoshiki (DUCKTAIL)
Illustration Sumimoto Nanami
Editing Amemiya Atsuko (Take One)

Translated from Japanese by HL Language Services

Distributed by:
North America, Latin America & Europe
Tuttle Publishing
364 Innovation Drive, North Clarendon
VT 05759-9436 U.S.A.
Tel: 1 (802) 773-8930; Fax: 1 (802) 773-6993
info@tuttlepublishing.com; www.tuttlepublishing.com

Japan
Tuttle Publishing
Yaekari Building, 3rd Floor
5-4-12 Osaki, Shinagawa-ku, Tokyo 141 0032
Tel: (81) 3 5437-0171; Fax: (81) 3 5437-0755
sales@tuttle.co.jp; www.tuttle.co.jp

Asia Pacific
Berkeley Books Pte. Ltd.
3 Kallang Sector #04-01, Singapore 349278
Tel: (65) 67412178; Fax: (65) 67412179
inquiries@periplus.com.sg; www.tuttlepublishing.com

Printed in Singapore 2109TP
24 23 22 21 10 9 8 7 6 5 4 3